A GARDENER'S GUIDE TO

Container
gardening

Editor Valerie Duncan
Series Editor Graham Strong

MEREHURST

Merehurst Ltd, Ferry House, 51-57 Lacy Road, Putney, London SW15 1PR

CONTENTS

Pots for every spot

As more people choose to live in town houses and modern properties with less space for traditional gardens, container gardening is becoming an increasingly popular option. Versatile and portable, containers allow you to create a mini garden wherever you live.

While container gardening is ideal for those with little or no space for a normal garden, it is far more than this. It is a very rewarding and creative way to garden in its own right. Any style of gardening can be reflected in a container garden – but on a different scale. It is quick, versatile and adaptable and allows the gardener almost endless scope to express their creativity.

One of the great appeals of container gardening, even to the most patient of gardeners, is the possibility of instant effect. Where there was nothing yesterday you could have a garden today. It is perfect, for example, for creating that special display for an important occasion.

Pots look particularly well grouped together *en masse*, and both plants and pots will contribute to the display. The different colours, shapes and textures can be mixed and matched to complement each other or to create contrasts for a variety of effects. Trying out new plants and new combinations of plants and pots is one of the joys of container gardening.

You can experiment with colours too to change the mood, such as a simple but elegant white and green scheme for a cool, restful effect, or a mix of hot reds and oranges for a sunny Mediterranean image.

And if you want a change of style, nothing could be simpler. All but the largest pots can be moved and rearranged, and this versatility is one of container gardening's great appeals, as well as being great fun.

With very few exceptions, it is possible to grow anything in a pot that can be grown in the garden – and more. Pots can be used to provide conditions that are different from the rest of the garden, allowing you to grow a much wider range of plants, such as lime-hating heathers in a chalky soil, or treasured alpines in a garden on heavy clay. And while container gardens do demand regular care and attention, there are compensations. There is no digging, little or no weeding, and pots are easy to get at so the plants can be given a little extra pampering to make sure they always look their best.

Growing plants in pots gives you the possibility of constantly colourful displays, as plants can be added as they come into bloom and replaced as they fade. By careful choice of flowers, complemented by trees, shrubs and foliage, it is possible to have year-round interest.

Groups of pots can be the answer for hiding many an eyesore in the garden too, perhaps screening an ugly view, or covering up that boring garage wall. And a group of mixed pots and tubs, surrounded by loose cobbles, could be just the solution for disguising that perennial problem – the manhole cover.

Containers are not only useful for self-contained displays. They can be used in borders to fill temporary gaps in planting, to incorporate tender plants in a summer bedding scheme, to lift a display that is looking a little dull, or to brighten a dark corner. They also give you the opportunity to experiment with new border plants, seeing their effect without disturbing the permanent display.

The opportunities for container gardening are almost endless, and can be adapted to suit all tastes and pockets. While you may not be able to afford a large stone urn, you can quickly build up a varied collection of cheaper containers, and for the really budget-conscious, anything that holds compost can be used as a container. You can find all sorts of discarded objects around the house and garden that can be recycled into containers for your plants at little or no cost. All it takes is a little imagination.

Patio gardens

Containers are an ideal way to bring colour and life to your patio. They will give you much greater flexibility in planning your design, and allow every bit of space to be exploited to the full. The dullest corner of the patio can be instantly transformed, and pots and plants can be mixed and matched to keep your patio looking good at all times. They can disguise an eyesore, fill an awkward corner, or create an instant effect. For example, just a few pots of bright annuals will bring colour to a newly-constructed patio while more permanent planting is established.

Containers in all shapes and sizes are ideal for breaking the monotony of large expanses of paving, adding colour, softening hard lines, and enabling you to create your own special style. Whether you prefer the look of a cottage garden, formal terrace, Mediterranean sun-trap, exotic Oriental garden or cool, green oasis, using containers will make it quick and easy to create the effect. And if you change your mind, it is just as simple to swop the containers around for a completely different style.

You can even change the apparent shape of the patio by moving containers to different positions, or you can break up a large featureless area into a linked group of smaller, more intimate spaces.

Tall pots, or climbers and other tall-growing plants, can be especially valuable in bringing height to large flat areas, dividing up the space, or creating instant screens.

There are many different ways

Bank up a wall of summer colour at the edge of your patio by placing a collection of pots side by side.

to make use of patio pots. The door to the patio can be made into a feature by positioning tubs on either side of it, filled with either formal or informal planting.

Containers could be placed at intervals around the edge of the patio, either defining a boundary separating the patio from the surrounding garden, or, by careful choice of complementary plants, linking it with the general garden. Pots can also be usefully positioned to mark the corner of the patio or the edge of a path or set of steps.

As patios are so often positioned next to the house, they can be used to create a visual link between house and garden, and this can be worth considering when planning patio containers. The different colours, shapes and textures of both pots and plants can be chosen to complement the decor of the house as well as each other to make a co-ordinating display.

The junction between patio

Herbs like parsley and golden-leaved marjoram provide a decorative and useful foil amongst bright bedding.

and house wall is one of those spots that can so often look bleak and bare and a few tubs filled with colourful flowers will provide a quick and simple way of brightening this space.

Unlike a permanent border planting, the pots can easily be moved if you need to get at the house for painting or general maintenance. Adding a few pots of climbers will add height and form and will quickly give a more established air.

CHOOSING PLANTS

Carefully chosen plants can make all the difference between a dull patio and one that is full of colour and interest. You can have potted flowers throughout the year if you choose plants with a variety of flowering times. The table on page 8 provides a general guide to seasonal flowers and foliage, although the precise flowering times will depend on the local conditions in your area.

While it is always a good idea to arrange your garden so that there is something of interest all year round, this is even more important when planning patios because they are nearly always sited where they can seen from the house and are therefore seen more frequently than other areas of the garden. It is therefore well worth making the effort to create a display that you can enjoy all the time, even on rainy days when you can only look out of the window.

As patio plants will be seen at closer quarters than most other plants in the garden, you will want plants that are looking their best. Container plants are ideal here as they can be moved onto the patio as they come into flower, and removed and swopped for something else as they start to fade.

Consider the aspect of your patio, and choose your container plants accordingly. A dark, north-facing patio need not be dull if you choose plants that will thrive in a shady spot, such as brightly variegated ivies and other foliage plants.

In contrast, a sunny south-facing patio will heat up surprisingly quickly and should be planted with drought-tolerant varieties if you want to keep your plants in good condition and cannot manage regular watering.

Houseplants can even be given a holiday and used to brighten dull corners of a patio when the warmer summer days arrive. Many houseplants have exotic flowers and foliage that can be used to add a new dimension to a patio arrangement.

If you use your patio a lot in the evenings, choose big and bold containers and plants with strong, architectural shapes that will show up well in poor light. Consider how colours appear in the low light at dusk too. Flowers in colours such as white and blue will show up well, while reds and purples, for example, will disappear into the background.

COLOUR

Colour is very much a question of personal taste, and while some may prefer a brilliant patchwork of colours, in the restricted space of small patios too many colours can sometimes look too 'busy' and can result in too many colour clashes, and it is often best to keep to no more than three colours.

More subtle, single or two-tone colour schemes can also work particularly well in the restricted space of a patio.

The choice of colour will have a great influence on the mood you can create. Hot colours such as red, orange or yellow are vibrant and will draw the eye and foreshorten a view, while pastel colours have a far more tranquil character.

Choose shades that will harmonise with one another for a restful effect, or those that will create a contrast for a more striking and exciting display.

Good use can be made of foliage too; the greens and greys of leaves are great harmonisers, balancing and softening the impact of the stronger colours in a display, while colourful foliage

AUTUMN	WINTER	SPRING	SUMMER
Asters	Bergenias	Anemone	Alyssum
Autumn crocus	Box	Aubrieta	Begonia
Chrysanthemum	Christmas rose	Azalea	Busy Lizzie
Cobaea scandens	Crocus	Bergenia	(Impatiens)
Cotoneaster	Dwarf conifers	Bluebell	Calendula
Cyclamen	Euonymus	Camellia	Campanula
Dahlia	Gaultheria	Chionodoxa	Clematis
Fuchsias	Hollies	Clematis	Everlastings
Heathers	Iris histrioides	Dianthus	Felicia
Japanese anemone	Ivies	Forget-me-not	Fuchsia
Japanese maples	Mahonia	Fritillaries	Geranium
Michaelmas daisy	Pansies	Grape hyacinth	Helichrysum
Ornamental	Polyanthus	Hyacinth	Herbs
cabbage and kale	Skimmia	Lenten rose	Hosta
Sedum	Snowdrops	Magnolia	Lilies
	Topiary	Narcissus	Lobelia
	Viburnum tinus	Periwinkle	Marigolds
	Winter-flowering	Polyanthus	Nicotiana
	heathers	Primulas	Pelargonium
		Rhododendron	Petunia
		Tulip	Rock rose
		Wallflower	Rose
			Salvia
			Snapdragon
			Strawberries
			Sweet pea

can often provide a longer-lasting effect than flowers.

Create new effects by planting different varieties close together and allowing the plants to mingle – the flowers of the different plants appearing to grow together, or the flowers of one emerging through the leaves of another.

SHAPE

Take structure and form into account, as well as colour, when planning your patio containers. A variety of shapes and heights will add much to the design and trailing plants always look good tumbling over the edge of containers, softening the outline and linking the container with the surroundings.

When planning your containers, consider how they will look from all angles. If the containers are to stand against a house wall the design only needs to be considered from the front, but if you are creating a free-standing arrangement, it needs to appear equally attractive from all sides.

An often-quoted general rule is to put the tallest plants at the centre or back, surrounded by lower growing ones, but equally effective displays can be created with an off-centre scheme. Do not be afraid to experiment. After all, a container display is so easy to change if you find you do not like the effect.

FRAGRANCE

A sunny patio can provide an ideal setting for scented plants as a warm position will encourage the release of fragrant oils which will linger longer in the sheltered air. Place a raised tub of fragrant flowers or aromatic foliage next to a favourite seat, or put pots of

scented plants near doors and windows so that their fragrance can be enjoyed from the house as

form an instant kitchen garden from which they could gather a few sprigs for cooking. Most

Geraniums are real sun-lovers and flower best when a little root-bound – but do not forget to water them regularly.

well as the patio. If you use the patio for evening meals and entertaining, you could also include flowers that have a stronger fragrance in the evening, such as night-scented stocks and nicotianas.

Patio plants are likely to be brushed against frequently so include some plants with aromatic foliage, such as lemon verbena and scented-leaved geraniums, so that you can enjoy their fragrance as you pass by.

A KITCHEN GARDEN

Keen cooks could group pots of herbs together close to the back door, or to a barbecue area, to

herbs grow well in containers and it can be an excellent way of keeping some of the more invasive herbs, such as mints, under control. A grouping of small pots makes a versatile arrangement that can easily be arranged to suite the mood – or the menu.

A FAMILY GARDEN

A note on safety should be added for those planning a display in a family garden. If there are likely to be children playing around the patio, make sure the containers are stable and secure and have no sharp edges, and avoid spiky, prickly or poisonous plants.

Balcony gardens

With a little care you can create a beautiful miniature landscape on even the tiniest balcony. Potted plants will help soften severe lines, add colour to an otherwise drab area and create a welcoming spot for relaxation. Experiment with lighting effects and you can also make your balcony a truly magical place to be at night.

Ideally, to make the most of your balcony, you should leave enough room for two chairs and a small table, and adequate space for pottering. Rectangular planters that can be placed along the edges of the balcony are good space-savers, as are hanging baskets and half-circle containers that can be attached to the wall. Try to use the largest containers that will fit comfortably. Small containers dry out quickly and will not provide adequate compost for good plant growth. It is far more effective to have two large containers with flourishing plants than a lot of small pots dotted about.

In planning a balcony garden, always check the structural condition of your balcony first, and consider the weight the floor of the balcony will have to bear.

Use lightweight containers, such as plastic or fibreglass, and spread the load over a wide area. Soil-less peat or peat

Decorative iron railings need only a few plants to set them off. Here succulents sit on the balcony floor and ivy geraniums are attached to the handrail.

substitute composts are the lightest, but you will need to check and water them more often, as they can be difficult to re-wet once they have dried out.

It is also important to ensure that surplus water can drain away. If your balcony does not have a drain, check that dripping water will not trouble neighbours on floors below or passers-by. Some containers come with matching saucers, but after watering you may need to drain off excess water from the saucers as many plants do not appreciate wet feet.

Strong winds and frosts can be a problem on exposed balconies, and you may find it beneficial to erect a sturdy trellis screen. This can also provide a home for climbing plants, although it could obstruct the view if not carefully positioned. Of course, this could be a benefit if there is an ugly view you want to hide.

When planning your plants,

Pansies look lovely when massed in a container on a sunny balcony.

remember that for much of the time they will be seen from inside. Choose plants to suit the amount of sunlight available. A sunny balcony is perfect for colourful annuals, succulents, herbs, miniature roses, summer bulbs and salad vegetables. If your balcony receives too much hot afternoon sun, you might need to install blinds or awnings.

A balcony that faces north or is shaded by nearby buildings is ideal for a large number of shade-loving plants. Lush foliage plants and white-flowering annuals, such as primulas and polyanthus, are good in shady spots and look wonderful lit up at night. Azaleas, fuchsias, camellias, busy lizzie (*Impatiens*), hydrangeas and daphne will flourish with some morning sun but shade for the rest of the day.

Evergreen shrubs and conifers, and climbers such as ivy, can be used to make a permanent scheme, against which background you can introduce seasonal displays. A balcony is a perfect place to

On this sunny balcony, a collection of decorative terracotta containers is used to show off petunias and lobelias.

introduce some fragrant flowers too, as their scent can also be enjoyed through open windows and doors even when you are inside. To make the most of the restricted space on a balcony, include some annual climbers which will rapidly give a backdrop of colour.

CARING FOR BALCONY PLANTS

If your balcony is high rise or in a very windy area you will need to choose sturdy, compact plants and low, squat pots that are unlikely to be blown over. Choose plants such as lavender, rosemary, variegated euonymus and box that are tough enough to withstand draughts and winds. (These plants will also tolerate salt spray should your balcony be near the sea.) Do not place hanging baskets in an unprotected

Geraniums are colourful container plants for any sunny position.

position where they will dry out very rapidly.

Plants in containers exposed to wind dehydrate very quickly and plants on balconies often do not receive the full benefit of rainwater because of awnings, guttering, a roof or overhead balcony. On hot summer days you should inspect container plants frequently to check

that the potting mix has not dried out, particularly in small containers. 'Self-watering' planters that have a reservoir of water for the plants to draw on can be useful, as can automatic watering systems. If a plant becomes very dry, take it to a sink and stand the pot in water until the soil is saturated.

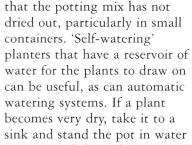

Windowboxes

Wherever you may live, nothing brightens the look of a house as much as well-planted windowboxes or hanging baskets, brimming with colourful flowers or cool, fresh foliage.

Although they are particularly valuable for town and city dweller who have little or no garden, windowboxes will enhance the look of any house, brightening dull expanses of brick and stone, lighting dark corners, softening hard lines, and creating an attractive and welcoming appearance that will bring pleasure not only to you but also to your guests and passers-by. Even if you put your windowboxes in the back garden where they will be for your eyes only, they can bring year-round pleasure for relatively little cost and effort.

To get the most enjoyment from your boxes, position them where you will see them most often, either at the front of the house where you will see them as you come and go each day, or outside a window you look out of frequently, such as that of the kitchen or living room, so that you can enjoy the display from inside the house as well, whatever the weather.

CHOOSING A WINDOWBOX

One of the first steps is to choose an appropriate style of container. The best windowboxes are those that are not there just to hold the plants that grow in them but to enhance their appearance. Unless completely hidden by the planting, they will make their own contribution to the display, and should be chosen to complement the window and the general architecture of the house as well as the plants. Consider the style and colour of the background against which they will be seen. An overly ornate formal box, or one painted in bold, brash colours would look out of place against a rustic cottage, for example. However, while many gardeners prefer boxes of simple, clean lines, in natural colours, there is lots of scope for those who prefer more individual designs.

If you are looking for inspiration, take a look at other windowboxes in your neighbourhood to see which styles you think work successfully, and to discover which plants grow well in your area.

SIZE

It is important that the container should be in proportion to the window and to the plants growing in it. The best looking boxes are generally those that fill the space available, so look for a

Give your window a complete makeover with a colour co-ordinated hanging basket to match the windowbox, and a climber to frame the scene.

Geraniums and verbenas always look bright and fresh against a white wall.

box that is as large as the window ledge will allow. If the box is too small for the ledge it will look lost and out of place. Large boxes are also more practical than smaller ones, as they hold more compost and more plants, and will not dry out as rapidly. And where the windowbox is easily accessible from the street, large, tightly-fitting boxes are less likely to be stolen than small, more portable ones. Avoid very shallow containers too as these will dry out very fast and need more frequent watering. The larger and deeper the box, the easier it is to grow healthy and attractive plants. Ideally boxes should be at least 20cm (8in) deep, and anything less than 15cm (6in) is not advisable for most plants.

If your sill is very narrow, don't feel that you can only have a very narrow box. It is quite practical for the box to be a little wider than the ledge or to be attached below rather than on the ledge, as long as it is well secured. If your sill is of an unusual shape or size, you don't need to make do with a hotch-potch of odd-sized containers as it is relatively simple to make a tailor-made wooden box to fit exactly, and this will be much more effective. An alternative is to make a fake windowbox, by fixing a 'front' across the sill, behind which you can stand containers of all shapes and sizes but still have a co-ordinated look from the front.

COLOUR

The colour of the box can be chosen to be a subdued background for the plants or to be a bold and integral part of the display. Boxes can be chosen, or painted, to blend – or contrast with – the background of the house. For a co-ordinated effect, the box can be chosen to match the paintwork of windows and doors, or to blend with the walls. This can be particularly effective where the box is fixed below the window and you want it to blend with, rather than stand out from, the background.

SUNNY POSITION	SHADY POSITION
Brachyscome	Ageratum
Calendula, dwarf	Begonia, bedding
Chives	Box
Chrysanthemum, dwarf	Busy lizzie (Impatiens)
Dianthus	Cyclamen
Felicia	Euonymus
Fuchsia	Ferns
Heliotrope	Forget-me-not
Marigold, French	Holly
Nemesia	Ivy
Pansy	Mint
Pelargoniums	Pansy
Petunia	Parsley
Rosemary	Polyanthus
Salvia	Primula
Silver foliage plants	Skimmia
Tagetes	Vinca
Thyme	
Tomatoes, cherry	
Verbena	

MATERIALS

The most widely available types of windowbox are those made of plastic. They are cheap, light and easy to handle, and they do not dry out as rapidly as other materials such as terracotta, but are perhaps the least attractive of the materials available. However, that said, modern plastics and modern designs are much improved and there is now a wide range available. If your sills will not take a lot of weight, plastic is often the best choice and requires less support.

Fibreglass is also a good choice where weight could be a limiting factor. And as well as being light in weight it is tough and long-lasting and can be made to imitate other materials such as stone and can be moulded into interesting shapes.

Stone itself is far too heavy for most windowsills, as are reconstituted stone, concrete and lead. However, if you have a position that will tolerate the weight, both stone and lead make very attractive, long-lasting and maintenance-free containers.

Terracotta troughs make attractive windowboxes, but are fragile and must be very securely attached. Make sure you choose one that is frost-proof if you plan to leave it outdoors all year round, and remember that

A windowbox display can be designed to blend in with the planting in the border below, either by using the same plants or by using a complementary colour scheme.

PLANTING BULBS IN WINDOWBOXES	
BULB	DEPTHS
Anemone	4cm
Bluebells	5cm
Daffodils	10cm
Dutch iris	4cm
Freesia	3cm
Grape hyacinth	4cm
Hyacinth	10cm
Ranunculus	3cm
Tulip	10cm

terracotta containers dry out quickly and will need more frequent watering.

Timber is one of the most popular choices for windowboxes, either leaving the natural grain of the wood to form part of the display, or painting and decorating it to match the surroundings. It is relatively inexpensive, particularly if you make your own boxes, and is light enough for most windowsills. One drawback is that wood has to be treated with a horticultural preservative or painted every 2 or 3 years otherwise it will rot. Although you can plant directly into wooden boxes it best to use a plastic liner to protect the wood.

ATTACHING A WINDOWBOX

Make sure the sill is structurally sound and will take the weight of the box, and freshen up any paintwork before you attach the box. Check which way the window opens, and take care to position the box so that it will not prevent it from opening.

Windowboxes can be positioned not only on the sill, but also below the sill or even above the window, as long as there is easy access to the box for watering and maintenance.

Whatever style of box you choose, it must be securely attached to the wall or sill. This is particularly important on

This windowbox is given added support by Fuchsia 'Thalia' rising up from a container placed below it.

upstairs windowsills, and where people will pass by beneath the box. When full, a box is very heavy and could cause serious damage or injury if it fell.

Even if the windowsill is deep enough for the box simply to sit on the sill, it is best to secure it to ensure that it cannot be knocked off accidentally. This can be done with safety chains, wires or brackets, or by a hook and eye attachment which makes it easier to remove the box for maintenance. Some sills slope, and in such cases wedges should be placed under the front of the box to ensure it is level. For a more decorative effect, ornamental 'rails' can be attached across the ledge in front of the box.

If the ledge is narrow or non-existent the box should be attached to the wall below the window with sturdy brackets. When choosing brackets, bear in mind the weight as well as the size of the box. Fix the brackets to the wall by drilling holes in the wall using a power drill with a masonry bit, and using wall plugs and screws.

PLANTING UP A WINDOWBOX

Position your windowbox before filling it with soil and adding the plants. Include only those plants that require similar amounts of water, fertiliser and sun and the same soil conditions.

Drainage is important, especially if a box is exposed to the rain, so whichever type of box you choose it should have drainage holes in the base. The box should not sit directly on a flat surface but should be raised up on blocks or small 'feet' otherwise water may not be able

to escape through the drainage holes. Make sure there is a good layer of crocks or other drainage material in the base.

Fill the box just over half full with compost. Soil-less, peat-based compost is best for fast-growing temporary plantings and is lighter and easy to work, but for long-term permanent plantings a good soil-based compost is better, as it retains water and nutrients longer. Position the plants and fill in with compost to about 2.5cm (1in) from the top of the box, firm well and water.

Don't skimp on the planting if you want a luxuriant display, but do not cram the plants in so tight there is no room for root growth. As well as putting plants for long-term or permanent displays directly into the box, you can also put pots of plants inside the box, packing peat or a lightweight 'plunge' material around them to disguise the inner pots and help keep the plants moist and cool. If you water the peat at the same time as the pots, it will also provide a reservoir of moisture for the plants to draw on and reduce the frequency of watering required.

Another advantage of using pots or removable liners is that you can

always have the next season's display growing on in readiness for when the present display has finished. It is then a simple matter to swap the pots or liners over, and you will have a display that always looks at its best.

CARE AND MAINTENANCE

To keep a windowbox looking good, it will require regular attention. Pick off all finished flowers and prune any plants that become leggy or straggly.

Water the plants carefully for the first few weeks until they are established. A light mulch will help to conserve moisture. Windowboxes dry out rapidly, so it is essential to remember to water: in summer this might mean every day. Aim to keep the soil just moist, but not soggy. Try to water your boxes when they are out of direct sunlight, preferably in the early morning or evening.

Windowbox plants will need regular feeding. Use a slow-release fertiliser for long-term plantings, or diluted liquid plant food for annuals and vegetables, beginning about a month after planting and continuing every 1–2 weeks. Do not apply fertilisers to dry soils.

This custom-made box fits perfectly around a bay window.

Tulips and pansies are followed by non-stop begonias and surfinia petunias.

SELECTING PLANTS FOR WINDOWBOXES

The key to a beautiful and healthy windowbox display is choosing suitable plants for your particular position. It is, of course, essential to choose plants that like the same conditions of soil, climate and aspect for each box. For example, which direction does the box face? Will it be in sun or shade for most of the day? In the box on page 13 are some favourite windowbox plants, listed according to whether they prefer a sunny or shady position. When planning your display, it can be helpful to look at other boxes in your neighbourhood to give you an idea of which plants are most successful in your area.

The plants chosen should be in proportion to the container and to the window, and should complement the house and the surrounding planting. If you have a border below the window, you may choose to echo the border planting in the windowbox, to choose complementary plants and colours, or perhaps to create a complete contrast.

Some gardeners like changing seasonal schemes, such as spring bulbs followed by summer bedding then winter heathers, while others prefer a fairly permanent year-round scheme based on evergreen perennials. Seasonal schemes can involve more work, planning and replanting, but will reward you with a constant succession of colour through the year.

Permanent schemes require less work but tend to be rather less colourful, although a careful choice of foliage plants combined with plants that produce flowers and berries at different times of year can also make an attractive year-round display.

If you have more than one box you can compromise by having both seasonal and permanent displays, or if you have a large box, it is possible to have a background of a permanent planting of evergreens to which you can add seasonal display of colourful flowers. These can either be planted directly into the box or to make it simpler to swop them over they can be placed in small pots which can

be exchanged for new ones as soon as the flowers are over.

Unless you particularly want to screen an ugly view from the window you will need to select low-growing plants that will not obstruct either the view or the light entering the room, or prevent the window being opened. Boxes positioned on the wall under the sill offer an advantage here, allowing you to grow taller plants without causing obstruction.

For many windows, therefore, tall plants are best grown to one or both sides of the windowbox. If you want to add extra height, climbers are also useful positioned at the ends of a box where they can be trained to grow up and around the window. The design should, of course, be tailored to suit the size of the window, larger windows being able to accommodate a much wider range of plants without causing too much obstruction.

Trailers, like climbers, will add another dimension to the display. Plant them around the edges of the box where they can drape over the sides, and either allow them to tumble freely for an informal effect, or keep them lightly trimmed for a more tailored look.

Summer bedding is still the most popular choice for a windowbox display and there is an enormous range of flowers to choose from, providing long-lasting bright colour, often from late spring until early autumn. There are plants to suit both sunny and shady boxes, and they can be used in many ways. A box planted with a single variety can have as striking an effect in its simplicity as a mixed planting where different types of flowers and foliage intermingle.

Colour, too, is an important consideration, blending or contrasting with the background of the container and the building. Depending on your personal taste you could choose a single colour scheme with lots of impact, a subtle blend of harmonious tones, or a vibrant patchwork of bright colours – they can all be equally effective in the appropriate setting.

Don't just rely only on flowers for colour though. There are many attractive foliage plants with leaves in colours such as silver, gold, yellow, cream, white, pink, purple or blue which will provide even longer lasting colour than the flowers. Colour theming with foliage plants can be especially effective in a winter windowbox when there are fewer flowers to choose from.

Foliage plants are also useful for adding that other essential, shape, to a windowbox design. Trained topiary specimens or spiky yuccas, for example, are perfect for setting off formal designs. Plants with different leaf shapes and textures can be used

For sheer flower power, line up hyacinths behind mixed winter heathers.

to create variety and interest. Low-growing foliage plants are also excellent for filling in around the base of the display, to cover the bare compost.

Even edible plants can be grown in a windowbox, from radish and baby carrots to colourful herbs such as variegated sages and thymes. A windowbox with a variety of herbs at a sunny kitchen window is beautiful to look at as well as very convenient if you want to pick a sprig or two while you are cooking.

Many herbs have a wonderful scent too, and fragrance is something that should not be ignored when considering windowbox plants, as the scent will waft into the house whenever you open the windows.

A final point to consider is that there can be a pollution problem if you have a windowbox near a busy town or city thoroughfare. Try growing plants that will

Spring miniatures in white and cream combine in a colour-themed display.

tolerate some air pollution such as ivies, rhododendrons and azaleas, polyanthus, dianthus and bulbs. You can help your plants by cleaning the grime off shiny-leaved evergreens, and making sure the potting mix does not become too acid.

Hanging baskets

Growing plants in hanging containers is a wonderful way to bring plant life to a height where it can be most appreciated. A suspended garden can also soften bare walls, hide ugly spots and provide plant interest at a number of different levels. However little space is available, there is always room for a hanging basket or two.

The traditional place to hang a basket is by a doorway where it can be seen whenever you enter or leave the house. A pair of baskets look superb either side of a front door and will create a bright welcoming effect, both for you and your visitors. They are as attractive by windows as they are by doors, and the planting can be planned to complement both windowboxes and borders.

But why stop at one or two? A row of well-filled baskets will look spectacular enough to stop passers-by in their tracks. Any bare wall or fence, shed or garage, will benefit from a display of hanging baskets, to brighten a boring area, disguise an eyesore, or create a link between different areas of the garden. Interesting effects can be achieved by hanging baskets from the branches of a tree, or, with free-standing posts and brackets, a hanging basket can be positioned anywhere you choose.

Filled with flowers, hanging baskets can be a spectacular sight in the warmer summer months and it is often assumed that hanging baskets are just for summer. There is good reason for this as the limited amount of compost the basket contains and its exposure to wind and weather from all sides makes it very vulnerable to freezing and to drying out in cold winter winds.

However, if you can give your basket a sheltered position, away from the worst of the weather, you will find that is possible to create year-round displays. While there are not as many colourful flowers readily available as there are to fill summer baskets, you will find that there are still plants that you can use in winter baskets, such as winter-flowering pansies, variegated ivies and small shrubs, and winter heathers, and the colour they provide is all the more welcome at a time of year when there is much less colour in the garden in general.

Don't forget to consider the practicalities when deciding where to hang your baskets. Don't hang them so low that you will bump your head on them, or so high that you cannot reach them. You may think they look spectacular by second-floor windows, but if you need a ladder to water and deadhead them you will soon change your mind. In any case,

You will need at least a 16-inch basket to recreate this profusion of petunias, blue scaevolas, begonias, bacopas and fuchsias.

19

This ball of Begonia semperflorens matches its setting to perfection.

you can enjoy your plants more when they are placed at eye level. Although you may be tempted to hang the container in a constantly sunny position, this will probably double its water requirements. Try to position it so that it does not receive strong afternoon sun during the summer.

CHOOSING A BASKET

The look of the container used as a hanging basket is in most cases of far less importance than with other types of container as the aim with most hanging baskets is that the plants, when fully grown, should completely cover the basket.

Once all that was available were wire baskets that we lined with sphagnum moss, and later fibre or foam liners. They were followed by plastic containers with drip trays. Today we can find a wonderful range of containers in a great variety of materials, from elegant dark green metal baskets to large flower balls with interchangeable pots. You can also buy self-watering hanging pots that allow the plants to draw

A predominance of lobelia and ivy-leaved geraniums give a light, airy feel.

exactly the amount of water they need from the built-in reservoir in the base of the container.

If your basket will show through the planting, choose one in a complementary colour and style. Some modern designs will even look decorative when empty and can be left in place between plantings. Unconventional baskets, from wicker baskets to old kettles and colanders, can also look very effective.

Baskets can be purchased in various sizes. Choose the largest that is practical (14-inch diameter and upwards), as larger baskets hold more compost and dry out less rapidly, making it easier to grow healthy, good-looking plants.

SUPPORTING HANGING BASKETS

When you select a hanging basket or wall container, give thought to its weight when full of plants and potting mix. Remember, too, that a container is going to take lots of water in the course of its life – think carefully about where you put it so it has adequate support, is easily accessible and will not drip on passers-by.

The most common and simplest method of supporting baskets is with wall-mounted brackets or hooks that have been designed for the purpose. Make sure that they are strong enough to take the weight of the basket when it is full of potting compost and plants and that they are securely attached. When choosing a bracket make sure that the arm is longer than half the diameter of the basket, otherwise the basket and plants will be damaged by catching against the wall.

Shop around to find brackets that are attractively designed, or at the very least will not stand out from the display like a sore thumb.

The bracket will need to take a lot of weight so make sure it is attached securely to a solid, flat surface with the correct length and gauge of screws. It is worth checking occasionally to make sure that the screws have not worked loose.

Heavy-duty hooks are also available so that baskets can be hung overhead from wooden porches or balconies. These should be strongly made with a metal plate to prevent the screws from splitting the wood.

PLANTING A HANGING GARDEN

There are potting composts available specifically for hanging baskets, although any proprietary potting compost can be used. If weight is a problem, peat or peat substitute composts are lighter, but don't forget that they are difficult to re-wet once they have dried out. Adding some vermiculite to the mix will help minimise the weight. To help retain moisture, mix some water-retaining granules with the compost before planting. A slow-release fertiliser can also be mixed in to avoid the need for weekly feeding.

To make planting easier, place the container in the mouth of a bucket or large pot to hold it steady while you are making up your arrangement. Line the basket with sphagnum moss or with a foam or fibre or other synthetic liner. If using moss, add an inner plastic lining, making holes in it for drainage. Fill the basket to about one-third full with potting compost and insert the first layer of plants. Make slits in the liner first, if necessary, then thread small plants through and anchor them firmly by packing more compost around the roots. Add more compost and more plants around the sides of the basket, planting up the top of the basket last. Add taller more upright plants in the centre of the basket, and trailing plants around the edge.

Do not skimp on the number of plants or the basket will look thin and unimpressive. In fact, it may be best to err on the side of overplanting when it comes to hanging baskets as they look most spectacular when over-flowing with flowers and foliage.

If possible, immerse the planted container in water for

PREPARING A HANGING BASKET

Stand basket in a pot and line basket.

Add a plastic lining or drip tray and some potting mix.

Remove plants from pots and place in basket, keeping root balls intact. Start at edges.

Add potting mix to fill air pockets, firming gently, and finish with taller plants in the centre. Water well.

half an hour or so to ensure the new soil is completely moist. Drain well before hanging the basket in its final position.

WATERING AND FEEDING

The limited size of hanging baskets, and their greater exposure to the weather, means that they tend to demand more care and attention than other types of container, and that they cannot be left unattended for any length of time. However, planted well, and regularly fed, watered and deadheaded, a hanging basket should look good throughout the summer months.

In the weeks after planting, water the basket regularly, particularly in dry, windy weather. Because a large number of plants are sharing a limited amount of compost, they will take up water and nutrients far more rapidly than in a larger container and daily watering may be needed on hot summer days. 'Self-watering' containers, with a reservoir of water for the plants to draw on, will mean that you

White trellis cut-outs make a clever frame for this free-standing basket.

need to water less frequently. Should a hanging container completely dry out it may be difficult to rewet the soil. Take the container down, stand it in a sink or bucket of water and allow it to soak for half an hour. It will then be well wetted and can be put back in position.

It is essential to position your basket where there is safe and easy access or you will soon tire of struggling to water it every day, and the display will suffer. Where the basket is easily accessible, you can take the basket down before watering and feeding and allow it to drain before replacing it. If a basket can be watered from a window or balcony, this will make the job easier. Various hose extensions and pump watering systems can be purchased from garden centres and shops to make reaching high baskets easier. Some baskets can be raised up and down by a pulley system which makes maintenance easier, but you should take care to choose one where the pulley

mechanism is easy to use and does not detract from the display. Perhaps the easiest system of all, if the most expensive, is to install an automatic drip watering system, linked to an outdoor tap. By adding one of the sophisticated 'water computers' now available, your hanging

Thoughtful planting and regular care will give you a stunning basket like this.

baskets can even be watered while you are away.

A couple of weeks after planting, start to feed with a liquid fertiliser. A high potash feed, such as tomato fertiliser, will encourage flowering, high nitrogen feeds are good for foliage, and a balanced fertiliser is best for mixed plantings. Feed weekly, following the manufacturer's directions. Only apply fertiliser when the plants are in active growth and when the soil is moist after watering. Alternatively, insert a slow-release fertiliser into the compost before planting. Check the instructions to be sure how long each type will last. Although many will last a whole summer, others will need to be supplemented at intervals.

PLANTS FOR A HANGING BASKET

Hanging baskets hold so little compost, and are dried out so quickly by the sun and the wind, that it is worth choosing plants that are tolerant of drying out occasionally.

The most appropriate plants are either those with a neat, mounded growing habit or those that trail. Upright plants, such as fuchsias and pelargoniums, can be grown in the top of a basket, but avoid anything that grows too tall. A basket can accommodate a large number of plants for its relative size and it looks all the better for being crowded. Pick plants with a long-flowering season to avoid the need to replant. There are lots of proven old favourites to choose from, including begonias, busy lizzies, creeping Jenny, fuchsias, helichrysum, ivy-leaved pelargoniums, ivies, lobelias, mimulus, nasturtiums, petunias, tradescantias and trailing verbenas. Decide whether you will hang your basket in sun or shade and choose your plants accordingly. Busy lizzies, mimulus, begonias, pansies and ivies, for example, are ideal for a shady basket.

It seems that most people still aim for a 'riot of colour' when planting their baskets, and certainly brightly coloured mixed plantings look stunningly effective, but single colour schemes can also look very striking, as can simple combinations of two or three complementary shades. Simple baskets of evergreen foliage such as variegated ivies can have a stylish effect and will last all year round. Consider, too, the background against which the plants will hang. For example, some colours will clash with bright red brickwork, and white flowers will stand out well against almost everything except a white wall.

Herbs also grow well in hanging gardens. Oregano, mints, thyme and prostrate rosemary are all generous spill-over plants that will soon cover most of the container. Upright herbs such as parsley, sage, basil and sorrel can be planted in the centre. Herbs can also make a very pleasing combination when planted with flowers.

BAGS, POUCHES AND SOCKS

The most recent additions to the range of hanging containers are re-usable bags, pouches and socks. Easy to use, they add another dimension to hanging displays. In their simplest form these are long, narrow bags made of strong, plastic with slits in one side for planting and handles at the top for hanging them up.

This basket is watered daily by an automatic pipe and drip system.

Flanking baskets and tubs and an overhead trough make this a very welcoming doorway.

Other types are more elaborate, allowing planting all round and incorporating a water reservoir. Simple but effective, they are filled with compost, which can be mixed with water-retaining granules and slow-release fertiliser, and planted through the slits in the sides with young plants of all sorts of summer bedding, and even strawberries or plants for winter displays. They can be hung anywhere a basket can be hung, and look quite spectacular when covered with blooms.

Creating a touch of class

Centred on a small clipped box, white and green plants are combined here to create a formal arrangement that complements the washed plaster container. It will look perfect on a balcony that opens from a formal living area.

PLANTING YOUR CONTAINER

This container should be planted in spring for a stylish summer display. Use a good quality potting compost and mix in some water-retaining granules. Choose a container to complement the plants. Our washed plaster trough measures 50 x 24cm (20 x 10in) and is 20cm (8in) deep.

Plant one small plant of box, two Lantana 'White Lightning', two senecio, two white fibrous-rooted begonias and three star daisies, all from strips or small pots. Apply slow-release fertiliser at planting time, following the manufacturer's instructions.

Place the container in a sunny position.

CARE OF YOUR CONTAINER

Water regularly to keep the mix moist but not wet. Pick off fallen begonia petals and decaying leaves to prevent fungus diseases. Cut back the daisies when necessary to keep the plants compact and to encourage new growth and flowers.

Alternatively, when they start to fade you can replace them with seasonal annuals, such as white violas or ornamental cabbage or kale.

THE PLANTS

• Box (*Buxus sempervirens* 'Suffruticosa'): The box is used for the strong shape of its dark green leaves rather than its flowers.
• Lantana (*Lantana montevidensis* 'White Lightning'): This bushy plant will continue to flower through the warmer months. It is also available in pale pink.
• Senecio (*Senecio cineraria* 'White Diamond'): The velvet-grey foliage is used to contrast with the other leaf colours.
• Begonia (*Begonia semperflorens*): The bronze, waxy leaves of this begonia will tolerate spells of hot sunshine.
• Star daisy (*Chrysanthemum paludosum*): A compact-growing daisy that is very suitable for use in containers.

BOX

BEGONIA

LANTANA

SENECIO

STAR DAISY

BUSH GERANIUM

PETUNIA

IVY GERANIUM

SWAN RIVER DAISY

IVY

Windowbox for a sunny ledge

This brilliant arrangement will brighten any

window and will quickly trail down

to conceal the container.

PLANTING YOUR WINDOWBOX

Plant this windowbox in spring or summer for flowers between late spring and autumn. Secure the windowbox to a window ledge that receives at least five hours of full sun each day. Use a good quality potting compost and mix in some water-retaining granules. You will need to select a container that is an appropriate size for your window ledge, and complements the style of your house. Our wire box measures 40 x 23cm (16 x 9in) and is 18cm (7in) deep.

Plant two bush geraniums, two ivy-leaved geraniums, two petunias, two Swan River daisies and two ivies. Apply slow-release fertiliser at planting time, following the product directions for amounts.

CARE OF YOUR WINDOWBOX

Water the box regularly to keep the mix moist but not wet. Avoid overhead watering of the geraniums. Pinch out the growing tips of the plants early in the growing season to encourage bushy growth and better flower displays. Remove spent flowers to encourage further flowering and cut back the geraniums and petunias if they become 'leggy'. Prune the ivy back as necessary to prevent it taking over the display. Keep a watch out for rust, a fungus that can be treated with fungicide spray.

THE PLANTS

• Bush geranium: This is a reliable flower if spent blooms are removed regularly.
• Ivy-leaved geranium: These trailing geraniums will cascade if grown well.
• Petunia: These will flower from June to September.
• Swan River daisy (*Brachyscome multifida*): The delicate blue flowers and fine foliage can be used to fill gaps.
• Ivy (*Hedera helix* cultivar): This small-leaved ivy is easy to grow in containers but is fast-growing and needs controlling if it is not to monopolise the display.

Cascades of colour

Wire baskets lined with sphagnum moss are light in weight and so ideal for hanging gardens. Some, like this one, are decorative too.

Sunny garden

PLANTING YOUR BASKET

Plant in late spring or summer for flowers from summer to autumn. This hanging garden requires a position in full sun with good air circulation. Use a good quality potting compost and mix in some water-retaining granules. Line a 50cm (20in) wire basket with plastic netting to retain the moss between the vertical wires. Fill in with sphagnum moss.

Plant two pot-grown verbena, two moss verbena, eight mixed alyssum seedlings and four petunias (two each of different shades of pink). Position the petunias in the middle of the basket. This basket is particularly heavy so hang it from a really sturdy support.

CARE OF YOUR BASKET

Water the container regularly, even daily, to keep it moist, and increase watering during hot and windy weather. The basket will look better if you also water underneath to keep the moss moist. Feed the plants every fortnight with a liquid soluble fertiliser, and keep a watch out for snails and slugs, especially on the verbena.

To encourage bushy growth on the petunias, pinch off the first flower buds on young plants, and deadhead regularly to encourage further flowering.

When the petunias have finished, replace them with star daisy seedlings. The alyssum plants can also be replaced as they finish.

THE PLANTS

• Petunia: Annual petunias come in a number of colours. Use a different colour each year for variety.
• Verbena (*Verbena peruviana*): This is a low-growing perennial with heads of small tubular flowers. It is very suitable for growing in pots and baskets.
• Moss verbena (*Verbena tenuisecta*): This low-growing perennial will cascade from the basket.
• Alyssum (*Lobularia maritima*): A fast-growing, hardy annual with tiny scented flowers. Various colours are available. For this basket, we chose a mixture in shades of pink and white.

VERBENA

PETUNIA

MOSS VERBENA

BUSY LIZZIE

LOBELIA

IVY

ALYSSUM

Shady garden

PLANTING YOUR BASKET

Plant in late spring or early summer for summer flowers. This basket has been designed to hang in a semi-shaded position during the summer months. It needs good air circulation. Use a 30cm (12in) round wire basket

The basket for the shade, as it looked soon after planting.

and the same lining and potting mix as for the sunny basket.

Cut openings in the lining just below the rim and in these openings plant ten white busy lizzie seedlings. Around the edge of the basket, just inside the busy lizzie, plant three ivy cuttings and twelve lobelia seedlings, and then in the middle of the basket plant six busy lizzie seedlings (three white seedlings and three mauve ones).

CARE OF YOUR BASKET

Water regularly, even daily, to keep the basket moist. A fine misting is also beneficial. Increase watering during hot and windy weather and keep the moss moist too by watering underneath.

Feed every fortnight with a liquid soluble fertiliser. Cut the busy lizzie back lightly to encourage new growth. The ivy, too, can be lightly pruned if necessary. If the lobelia starts to look tired, it can be replaced with small violas such as 'Princess Mxd' to give a new look to your basket.

THE PLANTS

• Busy lizzie (*Impatiens*): Low-growing busy lizzie varieties are ideal for containers.
• Lobelia (*Lobelia erinus*): The delicate blue flowers of lobelia provide contrast.
• Ivy (*Hedera helix*): Cascading streamers of ivy will soften the outline of the basket, but it needs to be controlled.

KANGAROO PAW

BLUE FESCUE

EVERLASTING DAISIES

FAN FLOWER

Garden for a hot spot

This elegant and unusual garden is based on tender, tropical plants. It enjoys the hot conditions many plants dislike, and will add distinction to any sun-trap area in your garden. The terracotta trough with moulded decoration is the perfect complement to the earthy colours of the plants. These plants flower from mid to late summer onwards.

PLANTING YOUR CONTAINER

Plant the container in late spring or early summer and place it in full sun. Use a good quality potting mix and make sure the mix is well drained.

To fill a terracotta trough such as the one shown, which measures 50 x 20cm (20 x 8in) and is 20cm (8in) high, you will need three of the kangaroo paws, three yellow everlasting daisies, three fan flowers and two blue fescues.

Some of these are hard to propagate and you will find that it is easiest to purchase young plants.

CARE OF YOUR CONTAINER

Water regularly to keep the mix slightly moist. You may need to water twice a week or even every day during hot, windy weather. Apply a balanced plant food, following the manufacturer's recommendations on the packet.

Water the compost if dry before applying the fertiliser.

Remove dead flowers as they finish to encourage new growth and further flowering. The flowering season can be extended considerably in this manner.

THE PLANTS

• Kangaroo paw (*Anigozanthos*): This tender, tropical plant will make an exotic container display in a hot spot.
• Everlasting daisies: Small, colourful flowers appear over a long period and will keep the container bright. For this example we have selected bright yellow flowers.
• Fan flower (*Scaevola* 'Petite'): This long-flowering hybrid cultivar has a tight growing habit, making it ideal for use in containers.
• Blue fescue (*Festuca glauca*): The blue-green leaves are used to create contrast both in shape and in colour.

Splendour in the shade

These bright pink and white busy lizzie plants are the perfect way to

brighten a shady corner, and the oval tin tub provides an effective contrast.

PLANTING YOUR TUB

Plant in late spring or early summer for a colourful summer display. Place the tub or other container in a light but shady spot. Use a good quality potting compost and mix in some water-retaining granules.

Choose a container such as the one shown, which is an oval tin tub with ten or twelve holes punched in the bottom with a nail for drainage. It measures 35 x 25cm (14 x 10in) and is 18cm (7in) deep.

Plant your container with three pot-grown busy lizzies, four floss flowers, three clumps of lobelias and four ivies.

CARE OF YOUR TUB

Water the container regularly to keep the mixture moist, but not wet. Increase the amount of watering during hot and windy weather. Lobelia prefers not to be watered from overhead. Feed once a month with a liquid soluble fertiliser.

Snip off spent floss flowers with secateurs and pick off fallen busy lizzie blooms to prevent them from marking the leaves. With good care this arrangement will continue to look good into late summer.

Don't allow the ivy to take over; prune it back carefully if it spreads too rapidly.

THE PLANTS

• Busy lizzie (*Impatiens* New Guinea hybrids): The new compact varieties now available have brilliant colours, and often colourful leaves too.
• Floss flower (*Ageratum houstonianum*): The small fluffy flowers of the floss flower contrast with the bolder blossoms of the busy lizzie.
• Lobelia (*Lobelia erinus*): Small patches of brilliant blue contrast with the grey tin tub.
• Ivy (*Hedera helix*): The small-leaved variegated variety is very easy to grow in containers, and will spread rapidly to trail over the edges of the tin tub.

The container when it was first planted. It looks a bit bare but the plants grow quickly.

BUSY LIZZIE

FLOSS FLOWER

LOBELIA

IVY

In the pink

This delightful spring display, colour themed around hyacinths in shades

that remind one of blackcurrants and strawberries, will look perfect on

a patio table or in a conservatory.

PLANTING YOUR TUB

Pot up the hyacinths individually in autumn, using a multi-purpose potting mix and putting each one into a 9cm (3.5in) pot. Use a few more than you will need for the final display so that you can select ones that will flower at the same time. Put the pots in a cool shady place and keep barely moist until active growth begins.

In spring, buy the bellis and pansies as individual pot-grown plants or in six-pack trays. Alternatively, you can raise them yourself from seed sown the previous summer in a bed, or better still a seed tray. Sow the pansies in a cool, shaded spot as they will not germinate in high temperatures.

Choose some suitable containers to plant up your display. Two nicely weathered clay pans have been used here. Assemble the display when the hyacinths start to show bud colour, and pack the plants in nice and tight.

For this display you can use six hyacinths and three pansies in the smaller pan, and eight hyacinths and five double daisies in the larger one. Fill in any bare spaces between the plants with moss. This will help to retain moisture and give the display a fresh look. Place the pans side by side for maximum impact.

HYACINTH 'DISTINCTION'

PANSY 'CASSIS'

CARE OF YOUR CONTAINERS

Water regularly to keep the mixture moist but not wet. Deadhead the pansies and daisies as needed to keep the display looking good and to prolong flowering. A liquid feed every two to three weeks is beneficial.

THE PLANTS

• Hyacinth 'Distinction': Distinctive and beautiful flowers, the colour of blackcurrants.
• Hyacinth 'China Pink': Following the fruity theme, these hyacinths are a shade of strawberry pink.

• Pansy 'Cassis': The colour of these pansies complements the hyacinths perfectly.
• Double daisy: For this scheme select a compact variety with flowers in shades of pink and red.

HYACINTH 'CHINA PINK'

DOUBLE DAISY

Suitable plants for pots

For many years we grew only a handful of trustworthy favourites in pots and yet,
if the right variety is chosen, there are very few plant groups that cannot be
grown well in containers – for example, you can create a beautiful
potted garden consisting only of edible plants, and some plants actually prefer
the special conditions a container can provide.

Flowers galore
Annuals, perennials and bulbs

Many colourful flowers can be grown in pots and they can be easily changed from season to season to achieve varying effects and colour combinations. Extensive plant breeding programmes have provided a wonderful range of dwarf varieties that are ideal for small pots, baskets and windowboxes, or can be tucked in around shrubs and trees in large tubs.

Some of the most popular flowers and bulbs are described here.

Agapanthus
Agapanthus need a sunny sheltered position. Grow them in well-drained compost, and water well in dry spells. They flower in mid to late summer or early autumn, and make handsome container plants with tall stems of blue flowers and strap-like leaves. Feed with any all-purpose plant food. Cut off dead flower stems unless you want to save the seed. Divide clumps in early spring. From seed, plants take about three years to flower.

The dazzling foliage of Amaranthus 'Joseph's Coat', a summer annual.

Watch for snails, which like hiding in the foliage.

Alyssum (Lobularia maritima)
Sweet alyssum is a fast-growing, spreading, annual plant flowering mainly in summer and early autumn. Sow seed under glass in early spring, or outdoors in late spring. Alyssum is tolerant of hot positions in full

sun, and becomes thin and leggy in shade.

Amaranthus
A spectacular annual for full sun and a warm, sheltered spot. Sow seed in early spring for a long summer display. Water and feed regularly during the growing season. Aphids can be a problem.

Anemone (Anemone De Caen)
Plant corms of spring-flowering varieties in autumn at a depth of 3–4cm (1–1.5in) for spring flowers. Anemones need sun. After planting and initial watering do not keep the mix too moist or the corms will rot. After plants emerge, water regularly in warm weather. Remove spent flowers to prolong flowering. They make excellent cut flowers.

Arum lily (Zantedeschia aethiopica)
Summer-flowering, frost tender perennials producing a handsome and distinctive funnel-shaped

The prostrate white Alyssum 'Carpet of Snow' in two tiers of pots.

Anemones are among the longest flowering of spring bulbs.

Arum lilies like lots of water – stand the pot in a full basin.

The bright yellow flowers of the twining black-eyed Susan.

Busy lizzies (Impatiens) will flower for months, indoors or out.

The butterfly flower is a rather delicate annual, best grown in a pot.

spathes. They prefer full sun or partial shade and a well-drained potting mix and need ample water in the growing season and some all-purpose food. Propagate arum lilies from offsets in winter. Snails can be a problem. The arum lily makes an unusual cut flower. 'Crowborough' is a good white variety, and 'Green Goddess' produces striking green spathes that are splashed with white.

Autumn crocus *(Colchicum)*
Plant corms in spring for autumn flowers. They need a sunny, sheltered spot and should be left undisturbed for about three years for the clump to multiply. Feed after flowering and do not cut down the foliage. Allow it to die down naturally.

Begonia
Bedding begonias will bloom throughout the summer in semi-shade or sun, producing colourful single or double flowers. The seed is extremely fine and difficult to handle and it is much easier to buy seedlings. Begonias need good drainage and regular but not excessive watering. They can get powdery mildew if too shaded and damp.

Black-eyed Susan *(Thunbergia alata)*
This annual twining climber for full sun is a moderately fast grower and flowers from early summer to early autumn. It can be grown from cuttings or seed, and needs regular water and fertiliser and a support.

Browallia
This tender perennial is generally grown as an annual, and is sown in spring for summer flowers, or in summer for winter flowers under cover. Seed should not be covered. It prefers full sun or at least a half day's sun, and a fertile, well-drained soil that should not be allowed to dry out completely. Feed regularly when flowering, and pinch out young shoots to encourage bushiness.

Bugle *(Ajuga)*
Bugle flowers in spring, but is often planted for its evergreen foliage colour as much as its spikes of blue flowers. A variety of foliage colours are available from metallic bronze to variegated pink and cream. In gardens it is used as a ground-cover. Bugle can be divided in autumn or winter. It grows in

sun or shade and any soil. Water regularly and give some fertiliser in warm months. Watch out for powdery mildew on leaves which can be a problem for bugle in crowded, humid conditions.

Busy lizzie *(Impatiens)*
Modern varieties produce compact plants in a wide range of vivid colours. They are ideal for pots or hanging baskets, and look best when several pots are grouped together. They are easily grown from tip cuttings taken in spring or summer. Impatiens are frost sensitive and do best in a partially shaded position. They need regular watering but will rot if too wet, and they should be fed with a liquid plant food.

Buttercup *(Ranunculus asiaticus)*
Plant the tuberous roots, claws down, 3–4cm (1–1.5in) deep in autumn for a spring display. Buttercups need good drainage (restrict watering until growth starts), full sun or part shade and wind protection. Water regularly in dry, windy weather, especially when in flower. When the foliage dies down, they can be lifted, dried and stored.

Celosias and French marigolds compete with each other for intensity of colour. Both enjoy a hot spot.

Dwarf asters, like these 'Comet Mxd', come with surprisingly large flowers. Cool them down with blue ageratum.

Blue spring-flowered clematis, like this C. macropetala, *can be snaked over shrubs like pieris to good effect.*

Butterfly flower *(Schizanthus)*
Also called poor man's orchid, this is excellent close-planted in baskets and pots. It prefers sun and protection from wind. Sow seed in spring for a summer to autumn display. Water regularly and feed as necessary.

Campanula
There are many species and varieties, ranging from annual Canterbury bells to the many perennial types. The low-growing perennial varieties can be grown in pots or baskets or as ground cover at the base of larger plants. They grow in sun or shade, but the flowers keep their colour better in shade. Some are propagated from seed, others from division of established clumps. Slugs can be a problem.

Celosia
Erect, bushy perennials grown as annuals, with conical feathery flowerheads in a wide range of colours. Sow seed in spring for a long summer to autumn display. They grow best on a sunny, sheltered patio. In summer give the plants regular water and fertiliser.

Chamomile *(Anthemis; Chamaemelum nobile)*
There are both annual and perennial varieties, with finely-divided, often aromatic, foliage and daisy-like flowers. They need full sun and well-drained soil and do not like a lot of fertiliser.

China aster *(Callistephus)*
The China aster is a fast-growing bushy annual with daisy-like flowers in a wide colour range. Tall varieties make excellent cut flowers. They need a sunny spot and wind protection. Tall cultivars may need support. Sow seeds in spring for summer flowers, feed regularly and give ample water in hot weather.

Chrysanthemum
Popular summer to autumn flowers in a wide range of colours and forms, they can be grown from root divisions or cuttings in spring. Chrysanthemums need plenty of organic matter to get the best results, and full sun and wind protection. Pinch out the growing tips when the plants are 10–15cm (4–6in) high and continue to pinch out sideshoots until the plants are large. You

can remove some smaller buds as they develop if you want fewer larger flowers. Fungal leaf spot can be a problem in showery humid conditions: water early in the day and avoid overhead watering. After flowers have faded, cut off spent blooms, repot and feed. Half-hardy types can be lifted and stored in a frost-free place over winter.

Clematis
Many clematis, especially *C. alpina* and *C. macropetala* types, make excellent container plants, as long as the container is big enough, as they make a large root system. Ideally, choose a container at least 45 x 45cm (18 x 18in) and fill it with good quality compost, such as John Innes No 3. Clematis need good drainage. Keep moist at all times and feed regularly, at least once a week, with a general liquid fertiliser. Provide your clematis with support, and it will reward you with a pillar of flowers in spring or summer, depending on the variety.

If possible, provide some shade for the container, as clematis like to have cool roots.

The compact Cosmos sulphureus *is also available in yellow.*

Cyclamen need perfect drainage and are valuable for autumn displays.

The early-flowering 'Fortune' daffodil is one of the most reliable.

Coleus

Decorative foliage plants for full sun, coleus may be grown from seed but are easy to propagate from soft tip cuttings taken in spring and summer. They need a fertile, well-drained potting mix and ample water in warm weather. Pinch out growing tips to encourage a bushy plant. Remove flowers when still small.

Cosmos

Sow seeds in autumn or spring, barely covering the seed, for bright daisy-like flowers in summer and early autumn. Plants need full sun and wind protection but are not fussy about fertiliser. Water well in dry weather. Pinch out tips to encourage sturdy growth.

Cyclamen

Cyclamen will bring colour to the garden in autumn and early winter, producing a succession of flowers, often lasting 2–3 months. Some have plain, heart-shaped leaves, while others have very attractive patterned leaves. Miniature cyclamen bloom as profusely as the larger plants. Give them a humus-rich, well-drained potting mix in sun or part shade. Water around the edge of the pot, or stand the pot in a saucer of water; do not water directly on to the corm.

Daffodil *(Narcissus)*

In autumn plant bulbs about 10cm (4in) deep. Restrict watering until growth starts. Plants need shelter but full to half sun. They flower from early spring to early summer, depending on variety. Feed after flowering and water regularly until foliage dies down. Plant out in a border as they are unlikely to flower as well again if kept in a container.

Dahlia

Colourful summer- and autumn-flowering perennials, offering a dazzling display of blooms in a variety of colours and shapes, with many patio varieties that are ideal for pots. Tubers can be over-wintered in a frost-free place and potted up each spring. Plant 8–10cm (3–4in) deep in a large pot, in a mix well enriched with organic matter. Unless dwarf forms are chosen, a stake should be inserted at planting time. After initial watering, water sparingly

Dwarf dahlias are the best choice for containers as they do not need staking.

Daylilies flower for a long summer season and are best in large pots.

Dutchman's purse like shade and warmth. They also do well indoors.

This is Rhodanthe 'Paper Cascade', a bushy perennial everlasting.

Floss flowers, felicias and lavender – a perfect mix of blue and mauve.

until plants are 10–15cm (4–6in) high. Then they should be watered and fed regularly. Tip prune to encourage branching. Snails can be a problem. Dahlias can also be grown from seed or bought as young plug plants.

Daylily *(Hemerocallis)*
The individual, trumpet-like flowers last only a day – hence the name – but are produced in succession over a long summer season. Plants do best in full sun and moist, fertile soil. While they are surprisingly tolerant of dry conditions, they respond to water in hot weather. One clump needs a 25–30cm (10–12in) pot. Divide clumps in winter or early spring.

Double daisy *(Bellis perennis)*
Many varieties with larger, more colourful flowers are now readily available. Sow seed in early summer, or divide after their spring flowering. Grow in sun or part shade in fertile, well-drained soil.

Dutch iris
(*Iris xiphium* hybrids)
Plant bulbs 4–5cm (1.5–2in) deep in autumn for spring flowers. Place in full sun and protect from wind. Be careful not to overwater in the

early stages of growth but water regularly when buds form.

Dutchman's purse *(Calceolaria)*
Compact, bushy plants with rounded, pouch-shaped flowers in shades of red, orange and yellow in late spring or summer. Most prefer a sheltered, sunny site with a gritty, peaty soil. Keep well-watered and protect against aphids.

Everlasting daisies
There are many varieties of everlasting daisies, which although more commonly associated with dried indoor arrangements, make excellent container plants putting on a long-lasting display of flowers. *Helichrysum bracteatum* 'Bright Bikini' is a good dwarf strain. It produces masses of richly-coloured papery flowers from mid to late summer. Trim off flowers when they are fully expanded to encourage more to develop. Rhodanthe is an eye-catching spill-over plant, ideal for planting in hanging baskets and around the edges of pots. It bears masses of small, papery white daisies that open from purplish buds. Sow seed in a very well-drained mix and be sure not to overwater. Give them full sun to flourish.

Fan flower *(Scaevola)*
Bushy, trailing, vigorous plants ideal for pots and baskets in semi-shade. Buy young plants from retailers or by mail order for flowers all summer and well into autumn. Give little or no fertiliser and water regularly in hot weather, but allow to dry out a little between waterings.

Felicia
A tender, bushy perennial, usually grown as an annual for its bright blue, yellow-centred daisy flowers, borne on long stalks from late spring to autumn. Sow seed or buy young plants in spring. Give felicias a sunny position as the flowers remain closed in dull weather, and grow in a well-drained potting mix. Water moderately as they do not like wet conditions. Deadhead regularly and keep trimmed back to prevent it becoming straggly.

Floss flower *(Ageratum)*
Hummock-forming annuals with clusters of feathery flowerheads from summer to autumn. Sow seed in spring and grow in fertile, well-drained soil. Deadhead regularly to maintain flowering and don't allow to dry out or flowering will be poor.

Forget-me-nots, loved for their soft blue blooms, will flower for weeks.

Short-growing foxgloves such as 'Foxy' are the best for containers.

Freesias look best with as many bulbs as the pot will hold.

Forget-me-not *(Myosotis)*
Starry blue forget-me-nots grow very easily from seed sown in summer for spring flowering. It prefers to grow in semi-shaded positions. The plants produce masses of sticky seed that will germinate wherever it falls.

Foxglove *(Digitalis)*
Grow foxgloves as biennials by sowing them in summer to bloom in early summer the following year. They prefer half shade and moist, well-drained

Ivy-leaved geraniums, here trailing from a tall urn, will flower for months.

soil, but tolerate most conditions. Give water when plants are starting to grow rapidly in spring. Snails can be a problem.

Freesia
Plant bulbs 3–4cm (1–1.5in) deep in autumn for spring flowers. Provide full sun but don't feed until after flowering and don't overwater. Support the sprawling foliage with a few twiggy sticks.

Gazania
The perfect plant for a dry spot, producing jewel-bright, daisy-like flowers over a long summer season. Sow seed in spring, buy young plug plants or divide existing clumps. Plants need little care once established but summer flowers are larger if watered regularly.

Geraniums *(Pelargonium)*
Geraniums (zonal and ivy-leaved pelargoniums) are easy to propagate from tip cuttings taken from spring to autumn. They flower best in full sun and will withstand periods of hot, dry weather. Sow seed in early spring or buy plugs or young plants in 9cm (3.5in) pots. Don't

overwater or use too much fertiliser as this encourages soft, sappy growth. Their bright cheery flowers are produced mainly through the summer but they will spot flower over a longer period and some have beautifully marked foliage. They are ideal for container growing and perfect for windowboxes.

Lanky growers can be kept compact by cutting back the stems by one-third or even more. Remove faded flowers to stimulate further blooms.

Plants may be overwintered in the greenhouse, cutting them back to 12cm (5in) and repotting.

Geraniums are prone to fungal disease and rust. Pick off the worst leaves, avoid overhead watering and water early in the day. You may need to spray with a fungicide. Watch for leaf-chewing caterpillars.

Grasses and sedges
Gardeners are increasingly realising the potential of ornamental grasses and sedges in the garden, and container gardening is no exception. Many varieties will grow very well in pots, and their long, arching

leaves are useful for adding an extra dimension to any design. They can also add extra elements of movement and sound as the leaves will rustle in even a gentle breeze.

Clump-forming grasses and sedges are ideal for pots, but containers also provide a way of growing some of the more spreading species which would be likely to over-run beds and borders in the open garden.

For long-lasting effect, choose varieties with colourful foliage; many silver- and gold-variegated forms are available.

Many grasses also have very decorative fluffy or feathery flower spikes that remain attractive even in the depths of winter.

Grape hyacinth (Muscari)
Plant bulbs 4cm (1.5in) deep in autumn for a spring display of dense flower spikes, usually in various shades of blue. They prefer a sunny position in well-drained soil. Restrict watering until growth starts, begin feeding after flowering and allow foliage to die down naturally.

Heart's ease are tiny wild pansies. They love half shade.

Heart's ease (Viola tricolor)
Seed can be sown in summer for spring flowers (it self-seeds freely), in sun or shade.

Hyacinth (Hyacinthus)
These fragrant and colourful flowers are amongst the most popular of spring-flowering bulbs. Often forced as Christmas houseplants, and excellent as spring bedding, they are also ideal for bringing colour and fragrance to any spring container display.

Plant the bulbs 5cm (2in) deep in autumn for a spring show. They prefer an open sunny position, or part shade. Restrict watering until growth starts and then water regularly. After flowering cut off spent blooms, feed with bulb fertiliser and water regularly until the foliage starts to yellow and die down.

Japanese anemone (Anemone hupehensis)
A hardy, branching perennial with cup-shaped soft pink flowers in summer and early autumn. Divide plants in spring. Place in shade or half sun and provide wind protection – although these plants are known as windflowers. Plants require little fertiliser but respond to regular watering in hot weather.

Kalanchoe
Available in flower for much of the year, kalanchoes will add bright flowers to outdoor displays of succulents. The kalanchoes like a half day's to a full day's sun and prefer to dry out between waterings. No special soil, fertiliser or other requirements.

Diminutive grape hyacinths give the richest and purest of spring blues.

Half a dozen potted hyacinths can be just as rewarding as a bedful.

Kalanchoe blossfeldiana *is available in a variety of bright colours.*

Kangaroo paw *(Anigozanthos)*

This exotic-looking flower requires a baking hot position and must have perfect drainage, full sun and good air circulation. Allow it to dry out between waterings and give little or no fertiliser. There are several good hybrids available, in a variety of colours.

Lamb's ear *(Stachys byzantina)*

This needs full sun, good air circulation and excellent drainage. It dislikes humid conditions. It is grown for its silvery foliage, but produces spikes of flowers in early summer if not cut back.

Lenten rose *(Helleborus)*

The common names of the Lenten rose and the related Christmas rose refer to the flowering times, but these do vary according to the weather and local conditions. They need shade, shelter and regular watering, but can live for many years in a pot. Clumps can be divided and hellebores self-seed readily. Remove spent flowers or any leaves past their prime. Snails can be a problem.

Kangaroo paws will make an exotic display in a hot spot.

African marigolds come in tall and short varieties, in orange or gold.

Lobelia

Popular for edging pots, where the trailing varieties will cascade over the sides, these are now available in white, pink red and mixtures as well as the traditional blue. Sow seeds in early spring for flowers through summer. Grow in full or half sun.

Marguerite daisy
(Chrysanthemum frutescens)

Easily grown from tip cuttings taken all year except winter, marguerites bear masses of daisies in spring, summer and autumn. They prefer to grow in full sun. Regularly remove the spent flowers to prolong flowering and prune the plants back hard after flowering.

Marigold, African and French *(Tagetes)*

Mostly flowering through summer and autumn, both African and French marigolds are readily grown from seed sown under glass in spring. They need a well-drained, sunny position for the best results. Regular watering and feeding and constant removal of dead flowers will help to maintain a long flowering period.

Marigold, English
(Calendula officinalis)

Sow seeds of this fast-growing, bushy annual in spring or autumn for a long flowering display of daisy-like flowers in shades of orange from spring to autumn. Grow them in full sun. There are single- and double-flowered forms and softer pastel shades. The dwarf varieties are most suitable for containers and are delightful with herbs and vegetables.

Nasturtium *(Tropaeolum)*

Sow the seed in spring for early summer to early autumn flowers. Grow the plants in full sun and a well-drained mix but don't feed them as this will stimulate leaf production at the expense of the flowers. Keep a watch out for blackfly which love nasturtiums. Caterpillars can also be a problem.

Nemesia

Sow seed in spring to provide flowers for summer bedding. There are also good perennial varieties. For the best plants, a position in full sun with wind protection is necessary.

Nasturtiums flower most freely if the soil isn't too fertile.

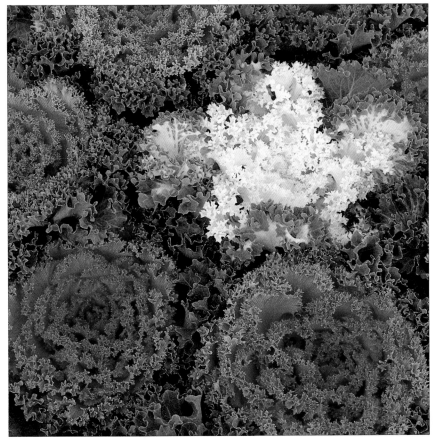

Ornamental kale has ruffled leaves, ornamental cabbages plain ones. Both do very well in containers and give soft colour for months in autumn and winter.

Pansies are old favourites for containers. They like rich soil.

Ornamental kale
(Brassica oleracea)
Sow outdoors in spring for a long-lasting display of ornamental foliage in autumn and winter. Give plants full sun and don't let them starve in small pots. Watch out for both snails and caterpillars.

Osteospermum
The bright summer flowers of the South African daisies do not open in the shade or on dull days, so these are plants for a hot, sunny position. Sow seed under glass in spring, buy young plants or propagate from cuttings of non-flowering shoots in summer, and grow in a well-drained potting mix. Water and feed regularly, and deadhead to prolong flowering. These tender perennials can be overwintered in a coldframe or greenhouse.

Pansy *(Viola x wittrockiana)*
As well as the summer-flowering types, winter-flowering varieties are widely available and are ideal for adding bright colour to winter containers. Pansies grow best in full sun. Regularly remove the spent blooms to ensure a long flowering season. They are easy to grow and have no special needs.

Periwinkle *(Vinca)*
This very hardy plant tolerates sun or shade but it flowers more freely in sun. The pretty blue or white flowers are produced from spring to late summer or early autumn. Propagate periwinkles from rooted sections of older plants in summer, or by division from autumn to spring. They have no special needs for water or fertiliser.

Petunia
Half-hardy perennials grown as annuals for their bright display of showy, colourful flowers through the summer. Petunias love hot, dry conditions, and hate wet, humid summers. The multiflora hybrids are more rain-resistant. For colourful, weather-resistant flowers, that are ideal for containers, little can beat the surfinia petunias. These vigorous trailing, free-flowering plants bloom from mid-June to autumn. Don't overwater. Few problems but snails love them.

Petunias are naturally trailing and thus wonderful for hanging baskets.

Polyanthus bear clusters of gold-centred flowers in bright colours.

Give portulacas sun; the flowers close up in shade.

An old garden chair will raise pinks and lavender up to nose height.

Phlox

Sow the seeds of phlox in spring for summer and autumn flowers. Give them a position in full sun or semi-shade. Plants must be well watered and fed during the growing season. Cut back hard after the first blooming to encourage sideshoots to flower further down the stems.

Pinks *(Dianthus)*

Annual pinks should be sown in spring, just covering the seeds, for flowers from summer to early autumn. Pinks need full sun and regular fertiliser. Don't overwater. They can be cut back after flowering but regrowth is often rather unsatisfactory.

Perennial cottage pinks can be grown from cuttings in spring and summer or from division of clumps in spring.

There are many named varieties that flower in late spring or summer. Many of the newer varieties are repeat-flowering with two or three flushes of flower in summer. They need full sun and very good drainage. A little lime added to the compost can be beneficial. Plants can collapse in wet, humid summers.

Polyanthus
(Primula x polyantha)

Growing polyanthus from seed can be a slow process, so it is easier to purchase plants in flower in winter and then keep them blooming through spring by picking off spent flowers. They prefer shade to semi-shade and to be moist but not wet. Watch for snails and give liquid feed monthly. Plants can be grown on for the following season in a shady position with occasional watering.

The long spikes of Salvia farinacea *bloom for most of the summer.*

Portulaca

Sow seed under glass in early spring and plant out in early June. The plants will flower through summer and autumn but they must have a hot, sunny spot; the flowers will close in shade. Don't overwater or overfeed the plants. Aphids can be a problem.

Salvia

Many types of perennial salvia are worth considering, including variegated herbs like sage grown for their colourful foliage as well as the salvias grown for their spikes of vibrant flowers. *Salvia splendens* is usually grown as an annual and should be sown in spring for its bright scarlet summer and autumn flowers. Provide a warm spot in full sun. Cut the plants back after their first flowering for a second flush of blooms.

Skimmia

Dense, bushy evergreen shrubs with glossy green leaves and clusters of red buds which make a cheery winter display. Clusters of small white flowers in spring are followed by bright red fruits on female plants. The fruits last

Statice is a tall grower and may need twiggy sticks for support.

Grow tall sweet peas up a tripod of light stakes, or choose a bush variety that will trail unsupported over the edge of the pot. Their scent is famous.

well, adding extra colour in autumn and winter containers but, except with *S. japonica* ssp. *reevsiana*, they are only produced if both male and female varieties are grown. Propagate by cuttings in late summer, and grow in shade or semi-shade in a fertile, moist mix. Too much sun or poor soil may cause yellowing of the leaves.

Snapdragon *(Antirrhinum)*

Usually grown as annuals for their spring to autumn display of colourful spikes of tubular or trumpet-shaped flowers. Sow the seed indoors in spring or buy tiny plugs or young plants in bloom. The plants take four or five months from seed to flower. Provide the plants with full sun and wind protection, and feed monthly for best results. Rust can be a problem in humid conditions. Water the plants early in the day and avoid overhead watering.

Statice *(Limonium; Psylliostachys)*

Statice seeds may be sown in early spring for summer and autumn flowers. They need full sun and perfect drainage, and

once established will tolerate drought and salty winds. The long-lasting summer-autumn blooms will dry well in the vase.

Sunflower *(Helianthus)*

Sunflowers are very easy to grow from seed sown in spring for summer or autumn flowers. They can be very tall and so need wind protection and staking. They must have full sun, regular water and monthly feeding. Watch for snails which can be a problem.

Dwarf sunflowers are well below knee-height and ideal for containers.

Swan river daisy *(Brachyscome)*

This bushy annual or tender perennial, with small, daisy-like flowerheads blooms in summer and early autumn and is good for pots or hanging baskets. It grows well from tip cuttings or from seed sown in spring. Provide a position in full sun, don't overwater and give little or no fertiliser. Cut back the plants after the first flowering to encourage bushy growth and continued blooming.

Sweet peas *(Lathyrus odoratus)*

Sow seed of sweet peas half an inch deep in autumn or spring for delightfully scented flowers from summer to early autumn. Seed can be soaked overnight before sowing to aid germination. Give a good initial watering and then restrict watering until the seedlings have emerged; water regularly once the seedlings are growing strongly. Liquid feed every seven to ten days. Plant in full sun, provide support and give wind protection.

Keep picking the flowers to prolong blooming. Dwarf types such as 'Bijou' are best for containers.

Verbenas are trailers and spill flowers over the lip of the container.

Clear-complexioned cousins of the pansy, violas are smaller in flower but every bit as prolific and valuable for containers. This is 'Tinkerbelle'.

Sweet William
(*Dianthus barbatus*)

Sow this biennial in summer for spring flowers the following year or under glass in March for flowers the same year. Grow in full sun, provide good drainage and don't overwater. Feed monthly when the plants are growing strongly. Remove spent flowers; you may get a second flush. Dwarf forms are particularly suitable for pots.

Tobacco plant (*Nicotiana*)

The flowers of the tobacco plant release a rich fragrance in the evening, and will bloom from midsummer until the first frosts. Position them near a door or window to enjoy their fragrance even when you are indoors. Sow seed in spring, and grow in sun or semi-shade in rich compost. Feed regularly or add a slow-release fertiliser to the compost. Dwarf varieties are generally best for containers, but check that the one you choose has a good fragrance as some dwarf strains have less scent.

Tulip (*Tulipa*)

Plant the bulbs 6cm (2.5in) deep in autumn for spring flowers. They need full sun and wind protection. Water sparingly until leaves emerge and then more regularly, but never allow the mix to be too wet. Pot-grown tulips rarely re-flower if kept in the container, but will often give a presentable display if planted out in the garden.

Verbena

Buy a collection of plug plants by mail order or buy larger plants in bloom in the spring. Clusters of small flowers on trailing stems make a bright summer display. Plant in full sun, with good drainage. Don't overwater or overfertilise. Watch for snails.

Viola

Sow seed in autumn or spring for flowers in spring and summer.

Tulips are brief in bloom; extend the season by under-planting them with annuals.

Wisteria is one of the strongest of all flowering vines, but pruning after bloom will keep it in bounds.

Pinch out the tips to encourage a bushy plant. Water regularly in dry spring weather and feed regularly once established. Remove spent flowers as they fade in order to prolong the period of blooming.

Wallflower *(Cheiranthus)*

Propagate by seed in summer or buy plants in late summer or early autumn. Wallflowers need an open, sunny spot but shelter from strong wind. The mix should be very well drained. Feed the plants about a month after setting them out. They will produce their fragrant, richly-coloured flowers in the spring. The plants should be discarded after flowering.

Wisteria

A very vigorous climber with long racemes of scented, pea-like flowers in early summer, it can be trained as a standard but will otherwise need a strong support. If it is to be grown in a container wisteria will require a large tub. The plant may need cutting back several times during the growing season and careful pruning after leaf fall to encourage flowering spurs. It should be given regular summer water but it is tolerant of a wide range of conditions, although it will not flower well in shade.

Greening your garden
Evergreens and foliage plants

Throughout the year evergreens can provide an invaluable background to show off the brighter seasonal displays of flowers, but foliage plants deserve more than to be used solely as a backdrop for flowers as many will make a very rewarding show in their own right. The different colours, shapes and textures of foliage can be used to give display that can look just as appealing as a floral show, though in a more subtle and sophisticated way.

Don't assume that all plants have the same boring green foliage. Just stop and think for a moment and you will realise what an enormous variety of shades of green there are, from the bright lime green of fresh new foliage to the deep dark green of the yew. And foliage is not just green. Plants have leaves in shades of gold, yellow, cream, white, silver, grey, brown, bronze, purple, pink and blue, and there are all manner of variegated forms as well.

You may not achieve the 'riot of colour' associated with summer bedding, but there are many foliage plants that will reward you with colour and interest all year round. This will be particularly welcome in winter when much of the rest of the garden is bare.

Evergreen plants also tend to be more shade-tolerant than many flowering plants, and are ideal for displays in shady areas where those with brightly variegated leaves in silver or gold will brighten dark corners. Alternatively, foliage can be used to make a more subtle display that is cool and restful compared to the vibrant colours of summer bedding.

Another aspect of foliage is the diversity of form and texture, and this can be used to add variety to a container display. Different leaf structures and textures can look wonderful when grouped in a container. Why not experiment and try out different combinations of smooth, hairy, shiny, matt, prickly, feathery, spiky, rounded, narrow, large, small, etc, to conjure up different moods, from luxuriant jungle to hot Mediterranean.

Plants such as lonicera and box can be trained as topiary shapes (see page 53) to provide an architectural element and give structure to more formal designs. Other architectural plants such as yuccas and phormiums can also be used in containers to make very effective designs, both formal and informal.

When creating a permanent or long-term display with foliage, it is even more essential to plan your display carefully. If a seasonal display doesn't work well, you can always try something different next season, but a foliage display is intended to be there to last.

It is especially important to keep plants grown for their foliage in top condition at all

You need a male and female holly to get berries, but those with variegated leaves can be grown for their foliage alone.

times, and for this you need to consider each plant's particular needs. For instance, some plants should be allowed to dry out between waterings and be kept fairly dry through winter, while others should be kept just moist at all times.

Many plants grown for their foliage do best where there is some reasonably bright light but little or no direct sun, although there are some, such as the silver-leaved plants and the sedums and sempervivums which thrive in hot sunny spots. So you need to get to know your plants' requirements.

All plants need regular water during the warmer months when they are in active growth but in winter they should be watered only often enough to stay just moist.

Do not feed during winter as the plants cannot use extra food during their resting period. Feed only during the growing season. Most foliage plants like to be given weak doses of liquid fertiliser regularly rather than a strong application once in a while. You may prefer to use slow-release granules that last three or four months. As it is easy for excess fertiliser salts to build up in the pot, it is a good idea to flush out the pots with clean water every few weeks. Stand the pot in a bucket or tub, fill it with water and allow the water to run through three or four times.

All foliage plants need grooming occasionally. You should wipe dust off leaves with a damp cloth or spray mist them with water. Cut off leaves that are starting to die so plants always look their best.

Here shrubs provide the framework and bedding plants the fillers, though the two spiky cordylines steal the show.

Popular evergreens and foliage plants

Ivies
Ivies are a great standby for container plantings of all kinds, and they really come into their own in winter as they are hardy and tolerate a wide range of weather conditions. Their climbing and trailing habit can be used to great advantage – they can be trained up supports to give height and structure to a design, they can fill in around the base of the planting, or they can be allowed to trail over the edge of the container to provide a soft edge to the planting. They are tough and fast growing, and may need to be regularly pruned to keep them under control.

For all but the largest containers, the small-leaved varieties are best. Try brightly variegated types, such as 'Goldheart', with a bold central splash of gold, or 'Silver Queen' with pretty cream-edged leaves.

Conifers
Dwarf conifers are also great standbys for container plantings. They are available in such a wide range of shapes, colours and textures that you should have no trouble finding one to suit any planting plan. Grown in a container, their diversity of shape and colour can be appreciated at close quarters, and being evergreen they provide year-round interest. The slim, upright forms are useful to provide a good contrast to the more bushy habit of other

Choose a variegated rhododendron for a centrepiece for winter and add heathers around the rim.

Leucothoe 'Scarletta' contrasts vividly with a yellow spreading conifer and winter heather.

Agave succulents sunbathe on gravel at the edge of a bed. A plastic pot can be masked inside a wicker basket.

shrubs, while the low and spreading forms will give good cover at the base of a container planting. Make sure you choose forms that are genuinely dwarf and will not outgrow the container in a couple of seasons.

They prefer an open site, but are excellent in containers as they need minimum maintenance and are tolerant of root restriction. They will also tolerate shady and draughty positions, but do not do well in areas with high levels of air pollution.

Shrubs and trees
A well-chosen group of hardy shrubs can produce a great variety of leaf form and colour. For all but the largest containers, it is best to pick shrubs that are naturally compact and slow growing or respond well to pruning. Larger shrubs will benefit from annual root pruning and repotting. They can be planted out in the garden once they grow too big for the container. Many small trees will grow well in

containers, the restricted space of the container limiting their growth. Choose those that have an interesting shape and branching pattern as well as colourful and shapely foliage. Amongst the many shrubs and trees to choose from are young plants of *Aucuba japonica*, *Pieris japonica*, hebes and variegated hollies. Euonymus are always popular, and there are many with boldly variegated silver or gold foliage to choose from, such as *E. fortunei* 'Silver Queen' or 'Emerald 'n' Gold'.

Dwarf rhododendrons and azaleas provide a fine year-round show of foliage, with the bonus of beautiful flowers. Some plants, such as the cotoneasters and skimmias, also have added value in the form of bright winter berries. But if you are choosing shrubs for flowers or fruit, avoid those that have boring and undistinguished foliage for the rest of the year.

Dwarf box trees and yew make excellent topiary specimens to add formal structure to a display.

Perennials
There is a wide range of perennials that will add foliage interest, from the bold-leaved bergenias and hostas, to the spiky phormiums.

Some of the low-growing or trailing perennial plants with colourful leaves, such as the ajugas, lamiums, vincas and lysimachias, will fill in well around the base of a planting to give any container a really full, well-clothed appearance.

Tender perennials such as helichrysums also make excellent container plants if grown as annuals for summer displays.

Grasses and sedges
Don't ignore the grasses and sedges; many of them will do very well in containers, and the long, arching shapes of their leaves adds an extra element to the design.

Try some brightly-coloured varieties such as *Carex oshimensis* 'Evergold', *Hakonechloa macra* 'Alboaurea' or the bright silvery blue *Festuca glauca*.

*Mahonia japonica or M.'Charity'
will both make a superb piece of living
architecture in a large pot.*

Ferns
Ferns love damp, shady
conditions and are perfect for
dark basements and north-facing
windowboxes. They offer a great
variety of foliage from glossy,
strap-shaped to finely-cut
feathery fronds.

Amongst the easiest are the
hart's tongue fern, *Asplenium
(Phyllitis) scolopendrium*, the
common polypody, *Polypodium
vulgare*, and various dryopteris.

Vegetables and herbs
Even edible plants can put on a
good show. Why not try
colourful herbs, such as the
variegated sages and thymes?
Most herbs respond well to
container culture, many have the
bonus of aromatic foliage and
some also add shape and texture,
such as the feathery foliage of dill
or fennel, the spiky leaves of
chives, or the deeply cut and
curled leaves of parsley. And for a
really bright, long-lasting foliage
display, you'd be hard pressed to
find a more obliging plant than
ornamental cabbage.

TOPIARY

To add a formal effect to
container displays little can
beat topiary, whether it is a single
specimen as a focal point, two to
frame a doorway, or a row to add a
formal elegance to paths or patios.

This technique for training trees
and shrubs has been used for
centuries to create strong
architectural and geometric
shapes. It lends itself as well to
elegantly simple shapes such as
cones, spheres and cubes, as to
more complex shapes such as
spirals and tiered designs and
humorous or informal designs such
as animals and birds.

Topiary shapes are perfect for
containers as they are compact and
attractive all year round, their
strong lines coming into their own
particularly well in winter. These
'living sculptures' make stylish
accessories with the added
advantage that they can be
positioned and repositioned
quickly and easily.

The best plants to use are those
with small, tightly-knit foliage
that recovers well from trimming,
such as privet and lonicera, as well
as the traditional box and yew. Bay
and hollies can also be trained into
simple shapes such as cones and
standards, but are more difficult to
train. For impatient gardeners who
want a more rapid effect, fast-
growing ivies can be trained to
cover a shaped framework. You
can create your own shape from
chicken wire packed with moss, or
buy one of the many wired shapes
available at garden centres.

While the simplest shapes, such
as cones and cubes, can be cut
freehand, it is best to use guides
and frames for these as well as the
more complex shapes. This gives a
shape to cut to and allows shoots
to be tied in where necessary.

*A classically decorated terracotta pot
is perfect for this clipped box cone.*

With topiary, patience is a great
virtue as, unless you purchase a
ready-trained specimen, it will
take several years to establish any
but the simplest shapes.

When initially forming the
shape take a lot of time and care
with the clipping. Work from the
top down and the centre out, and
don't take too much out of any
place at once, as it may take the
plant a long time to recover.

Once the shape is established, it
will need frequent trimming to
maintain, the timing depending on
the plant's rate of growth. Fast-
growing lonicera will need
trimming much more frequently
than the slower-growing yew. To
keep a well-defined shape it may
be necessary to trim fast-growing
plants every 4–6 weeks during the
growing season. Avoid clipping in
autumn and winter as this will
make the plant more vulnerable to
damage by winter weather.

To keep topiary healthy feed and
water the plants regularly during
the growing season. Turn the
container frequently to encourage
even growth.

Home-grown and healthy
Herbs and vegetables

HERBS

You can add a pleasant fragrance to your surroundings and a distinctive flavour to your cooking with herbs. Most herbs grow well in containers and they will thrive where they receive plenty of sunshine. A herb box is ideal for a sunny kitchen windowsill or you may have a sunny spot for a potted herb garden just outside the kitchen door. If all you can offer your herbs is a shady spot, try growing sorrel and mint. Parsley, chervil and watercress will grow in partial shade and rather damp conditions.

Parsley, chives, mint, sage, thyme, rosemary and basil are most often grown for their leaves. The seeds of anise, caraway, dill and coriander are also used in cooking.

Bay trees are especially attractive as container plants. Two neatly clipped bays in identical pots look stunning either side of an entrance, on a balcony or beside a back door; or you can give the surrounds of a pool or formal water feature a delightfully Mediterranean feel with a row of bay trees in identical terracotta pots. Rosemary, lavender and santolina also look wonderful when clipped in a formal manner.

Herbs can be grown in individual pots or several can be planted together in a large tub or hanging basket. Herbs which have a tendency to trail, such as thyme and prostrate rosemary, can be planted at the side of a large container, with upright

A grouping of vegetables, herbs and flowers in a variety of containers makes an attractive display.

herbs, such as basil, sage, hyssop or upright rosemary, in the middle.

Herbs need a good potting mix and good drainage. Water the plants well whenever they feel dry just below the surface. Watering twice a day may be necessary during a windy or hot spell in summer for soft herbs such as basil, mint and parsley. However, as most of the culinary herbs are of Mediterranean origin, they prefer to dry out between waterings. Take care not to overwater as it is very easy to kill herbs such as sage, thyme, oregano and rosemary by keeping them constantly moist.

Raising herbs from seed

Many herbs grow well from seed, and packets of seed are available from most garden centres and large supermarkets. You can start seeds in any clean, flat container

with adequate drainage. Plastic seed trays are ideal and easy to wash clean. Use a commercial seed-raising compost based on peat or on a peat substitute.

Fill the container to within 1.25cm (0.5in) of the top and firm down the mixture. Gently sprinkle a few seeds over the surface of the compost and lightly press them in so that the seeds come into good contact with the compost. Finally add a light sprinkling of compost on top of the seeds.

Water the container carefully with a fine spray. Alternatively, soak the bottom of the container in a dish filled with water so that moisture will be drawn up into the soil by capillary action. When the soil is completely moist, lift the container out of the dish and leave it to drain. Keep the soil damp, but not wet, until seedlings emerge. This may be within a week for fast germinating seeds but could take up to six weeks for parsley.

Once the seedlings have developed a few leaves and a small root system they can be transplanted into another seed tray, carefully spaced out, or into your display pot.

Fill the tray or pot with potting mixture and make a hole in the mix with your finger, just big enough to take the seedling. Lower the seedling gently into the hole and press the soil mixture around the roots.

Gently water the seedlings in – this will also settle the soil around the roots. It is always best to transplant seedlings in the cool of the day.

You can grow a complete herb garden in a windowbox, but remember that most herbs are sun lovers. From left: purple basil, parsley, rosemary, thymes, dandelions and oregano, with a viola for colour.

VEGETABLES

Providing you give them plenty of sunlight, many vegetables can be grown successfully in containers. Apart from providing you with fresh pickings, well-grown vegetables in pots can be extremely beautiful.

Seed companies now supply a wonderful range of space-saving compact plants, and this makes the choice of what to plant more interesting. These compact plants include baby beets, dwarf beans, baby and round carrots and golf-ball-sized turnips. Lettuce, radish, Swiss chard, capsicums and tomatoes are also suitable for growing in pots. For a really small potted vegetable garden it may be easier to buy punnets of mixed seedlings such as lettuce or mixed salad leaves. When sowing your own, it is best to make successive small plantings, say every three weeks, if you want to ensure continuous cropping of vegetables.

Lettuces, radishes, beetroot and Swiss chard have fairly shallow roots and grow well in boxes or toughs up to 20cm (8in) deep. Larger vegetables, such as tomatoes, capsicums and courgettes, will need deeper pots. Root crops need a minimum depth of 25cm (10in).

The gardener with only a small space can take advantage of wall space by growing beans, cucumbers and tomatoes in planter boxes or tubs against a wall. Position the containers against a support such as wire mesh or trelliswork and tie the developing stems to the support as they become taller.

Growing conditions

Make sure all containers used for growing vegetables have adequate drainage holes. A good commercial potting mix suits most vegetables, but add a slow-release granular complete plant food to the container before planting. The soil should come within 2.5cm (1in) of the container top when the mixture has settled down. Top it up if necessary.

Keep plants growing rapidly by regularly applying fertiliser. Leafy vegetables such as lettuce and Swiss chard, can be fed every fortnight with a soluble fertiliser.

Never let the plants suffer from lack of moisture. Water whenever the soil feels dry just below the surface: this may be twice a day in hot, dry weather. Always water thoroughly and make sure the water has soaked down to the root areas. A mulch of dried lawn clippings, gravel, compost or peat moss will help reduce evaporation.

Popular herbs and vegetables

These are some of the most popular herbs and vegetables for containers.

Anise (Pimpinella anisum)
Sow seeds of this annual herb in spring in a well-drained mix. Anise needs full sun and regular water but allow it to dry out (but not wilt) between waterings. Harvest the seeds in autumn; hang stems to dry, then remove the dried seed and store it in an airtight container.

Basil (Ocimum basilicum)
Sow basil from late spring to early summer in a greenhouse or a windowsill indoors. Grow it in full sun, and water and feed the plants regularly. Don't allow it to flower too early or growth will cease. Pinch out growing tips often for bushy plants. Snails and some caterpillars love basil.

Bay (Laurus nobilis)
Bay trees in the open ground grow into very large trees, but you can grow one in a container for many years. It strikes readily from cuttings taken in late summer. Bay is fairly slow growing and can be trimmed to a formal shape or left to develop its own neat style. Bay trees are not fully hardy when grown in pots and hate cold, drying winds that can turn the leaves brown. Move them under a warm wall or indoors in winter.

Plant bay trees in full sun, in a well-drained mix, but be sure to give them plenty of water in warm weather. Leaves can be picked for the kitchen as required. If your plant is attacked by scale insects, treat it with an insecticidal soap spray.

Basil and tomatoes; good companions in the garden and in the kitchen.

Beans (Phaseolus)
Sow beans under cover in early spring or outdoors when danger of frost has passed. The potting mix should be moist when sowing. Water thoroughly after sowing, and then do not water again until the seedlings emerge, unless the mix looks like drying out completely. Supports are needed for climbing beans. Grow

The bay tree is a slow grower, and happy to live in a large container.

them in full sun, and feed and water regularly throughout the growing season. Once the beans have started cropping, pick them every few days to encourage a longer cropping season.

Aphids, red spider mites and bean fly are the main pests that trouble beans; they can be controlled by spraying with insecticides, especially on the undersides of the leaves.

Beetroot (Beta vulgaris)
Globe-rooted types of beetroot can be grown in large containers, especially the newer mini varieties. Before sowing, place a complete plant food about 10cm (4in) from the top of the pot, refill the pot with potting mix and sow seeds about 10cm (4in) apart in spring or summer. Restrict watering until the seedlings emerge, and then water and feed regularly. The roots will emerge at the surface; do not cover them.

Capsicum (Capsicum annuum)
Sow seed of capsicums, or sweet peppers, in early spring under glass. From seed they will take five to six months to produce fruit. They need regular water, fertiliser, full sun and shelter. However, do not keep the mix soggy or root rot will occur. Plants can be affected by many of the tomato pests and diseases, including white fly.

Caraway (Carum carvi)
Sow the seeds of caraway in early spring and give the plants full sun. Wind protection is also needed as this light, airy herb grows 60–90cm (2–3ft) tall. Water the plants regularly but

An unusual 'basket' of 'Borlotto' and 'Purple Teepee' beans with red lettuce.

Chives have attractive mauve flowers and are easy to grow in containers.

A sunny windowsill in the kitchen is an ideal spot for a collection of herbs.

don't keep them wet. When the seeds are ripe, cut off the seedheads and dry them thoroughly before storing the seeds in an airtight container.

Carrots (*Daucus carota*)

Baby carrots are best for containers because of the restricted soil depth. Don't add extra fertiliser to the mix or the roots will fork. Cover the fine sown seed with sand to avoid surface caking and thin out the seedlings as required. Sow seed from spring to early summer. Full sun, good drainage and ample water in hot weather are needed. They take four to five months to reach maturity but young carrots can be pulled and eaten at any time. Carrot root fly can be a problem.

Chamomile (*Anthemis nobilis; Matricaria chamomilla*)

There are both annual and perennials types of chamomile, but seed of all varieties can be sown in spring. They prefer full sun, but will grow in partial shade, and need regular water and good drainage. Pick flowerheads on a warm, dry day and spread them to dry.

Chervil (*Anthriscus cerefolium*)

Sow the seeds in spring, preferably where they are to grow as they do not like transplanting. Chervil enjoys dappled shade and will quickly run to seed in hot, dry conditions. Give it plenty of water in summer. Leaves can be picked as required, or clip them before flowering and hang to dry.

Chives (*Allium schoenoprasum*)

Chives can be grown from seed sown in spring or summer, but

Chamomile flowers, just waiting to be gathered and dried.

propagation is easiest from division of old clumps in late winter, when plants are still fairly dormant. Full sun and a regular supply of water and fertiliser will ensure a good supply of tasty leaves for many months. Chives are rarely attacked by insects; although aphids can be a problem for pot-grown plants.

Coriander (*Coriandrum sativum*)

Seed can be sown from spring to early summer. Coriander requires full sun, wind protection and regular water to maintain growth. Too rich a soil lessens the flavour. It may need staking. Leaves can be picked often, but don't denude the plant. Seeds can be collected when dry and ripe.

Cucumber (*Cucumis sativus*)

There are small types, available as seed, which are suitable for container growing. Sow seeds in 9cm (3.5in) pots in a warm propagator or on a windowsill above a radiator. Water and feed regularly for quick growth and good fruit. Powdery mildew can be a problem.

Dill *(Anethum graveolens)*

Sow seeds from spring to early summer. Dill needs full sun, wind protection and possibly staking or support. Allow the mix to dry out between waterings but keep the plant growing quickly. Leaves can be picked as required but seedheads should ripen on the plant before being picked and dried completely.

Lavender *(Lavandula)*

Lavender must have full sun and good drainage to thrive. Although it can be grown from seed, it is best grown from cuttings taken in summer. Plants can grow quite large and will need repotting as they outgrow the smaller pots. Allow to dry out between waterings and give little or no fertiliser. Pick the blooms or trim back lightly after flowering.

Compact French lavender between two bushes of the English type.

Lemon grass. The soft bases of the leaves are used in Asian cooking.

Lemon grass *(Cymbopogon citratus)*

A tender perennial, this is unlikely to survive the winter in borders and is best grown in a container which can be overwintered in a warm greenhouse or conservatory. New plants can be started in spring by cutting a few fleshy stalks from a clump below soil level. Make sure each piece has a root attached to it. It is sometimes easier to remove the plant from its pot and divide it, and then replant the separate pieces. It is also possible to strike a piece bought at the supermarket. Look for a piece that is fresh and has a good fleshy base. Insert it directly in a moist potting mix and keep the pot in a warm, shady place. Roots should form within two or three weeks.

Lettuce *(Lactuca sativa)*

It is important to choose the right variety for the season of planting. Lettuce must be grown quickly with regular water and fertiliser applied every ten to 14 days. Make successive sowings so that you do not have all your lettuces maturing at once. Most lettuces will quickly go to seed in very hot weather. Watch out for snails and slugs, which are the worst threats.

Mint *(Mentha)*

Mint will grow in a semi-shady spot in moist potting mix. Any piece of root will grow and it can become invasive in the garden, so it is best grown in a container. It can be cut back hard to get fresh, young shoots, and will die down in winter. Keep it well watered throughout the growing season. Caterpillars chew the leaves and rust can be a problem.

Seed packs of salad leaves allow a constant supply for salads. Pick a few leaves at a time as they are needed.

Red-leaved lettuce, parsley and golden marjoram are a feast for the eyes as well as the taste buds.

If rust occurs, remove affected leaves or pull out the plant if it is too bad.

Oregano *(Origanum vulgare)*

Oregano prefers full sun or partial shade. Gold-leaved varieties may scorch in full sun and are best given some shade. A perennial herb, it can be grown from seed sown in spring or from division or cuttings in late spring and summer. Plants need regular cutting back, and become woody after three or four years and are best started again. Allow the mix to dry out between waterings, and give the plants little or no fertiliser.

Parsley *(Petroselinum)*

Sow seed in spring and summer. It can be slow to germinate and must be kept moist at all times. Parsley prefers sun but will tolerate light shade. Italian parsley is much faster to germinate and may take only a few days. Keep the soil moist; do not let it dry out in hot weather. Occasional feeds of a nitrogen-rich fertiliser will promote more leaf growth. Although parsley is strictly a biennial, it is best treated as an annual and replanted each year.

There are several varieties of rosemary, both bush and prostrate.

Radish *(Raphanus sativus)*

Radishes can be grown from early spring to late summer and are quick to mature. Put some complete fertiliser in the potting mix before sowing the seed direct. Plants can be thinned out after germination. They need full sun or light shade and plenty of water, and have a tendency to bolt in hot weather. Sow every four to six weeks to ensure a continuous supply.

Rocket *(Eruca vesicaria ssp. sativa)*

Sow seeds of this fast-growing annual from early spring to mid-summer. Rocket resents heat and likes some shade and regular water and fertiliser. Plants can be quite tall and so are best given wind protection. Leaves will be ready to pick within 6–8 weeks of sowing and can be picked as needed – keep the pot near the kitchen door.

Rosemary *(Rosmarinus officinalis)*

Grown from cuttings taken from late spring to early autumn, rosemary needs perfect drainage and full sun. Lime added to the mix is beneficial. Allow it to dry out between waterings and be careful not to overwater in winter. Cut sprigs for fragrance or culinary use, and cut bushes back after flowering in spring to maintain compact growth. Plants can become large and will need potting on to larger containers as they grow.

Sage *(Salvia officinalis)*

Sage must have a very free-draining potting mix and will not tolerate 'wet feet' at any stage. It must have full sun, too. Plants can be grown from seed in spring and from cuttings taken in late spring or autumn. Water regularly until the plants are established, but then only if the soil is dry – sage will not survive damp conditions.

Pick leaves as they are needed or pick young ones before flowering and dry them in a dark, airy place.

Santolina

The aromatic, silver-leaved cotton lavender needs full sun and perfect drainage to grow well. Grown from cuttings taken either in late spring or in autumn, the plants can be spreading and should be regularly cut back to keep them compact. Usually grown for its

Golden sage growing amongst beans, basil, rosemary and golden marjoram.

This wicker basket hanging outside a kitchen door holds a collection of herbs.

silvery foliage, you may prefer to let cotton lavender produce its bright yellow summer flowers before cutting it back.

Sorrel *(Rumex scutatus)*

Sow the seed in spring or divide the roots of existing clumps in

autumn or early spring. Sorrel prefers full sun but tolerates semi-shade. It needs regular water in hot weather and occasional fertiliser. As the flower stalks appear in summer, remove them at the base or plant growth will stop. Snails and slugs can

STRAWBERRIES

Even the smallest garden has room for strawberries (*Fragaria*). They are one of the easiest crops to grow in containers and will produce their beautiful sweet fruit from early through to late summer, depending on the variety.

Suitable containers for strawberries include barrels, strawberry pots or specially designed plastic bins with many holes in the sides. The plants are inserted through the holes into a good rich soil inside the barrel.

Use a proprietary potting compost into which you can incorporate a slow-release granular fertiliser to give season-long feeding.

High-yielding and certified virus-free new plants

can be bought from garden centres and specialist nurseries. Plants will send out runners that eventually take root and form new plants. When these develop they can be transplanted carefully into a good rich soil. The best runners are those taken from plants that have not yet fruited.

It is a good plan to start some new strawberry plants each year as a strawberry's productive life is only two or three years.

Grey mould is a serious fungal disease that will rot strawberries. To avoid it, position your pots in an open, sunny spot with some protection from wind, and avoiding watering late in the day.

The best tomatoes for containers are the small 'cherry' tomatoes.

Choose compact types of zucchini (courgettes) to grow in containers.

cause damage. If leaf miners attack the plant, remove and destroy affected leaves.

Swiss chard
(Beta vulgaris var. cicla)
Swiss chard can be grown from seed sown from spring to summer. The plants need full sun or part shade and regular watering and fertiliser. Swiss chard crops over a long period; pick the leaves as needed by cutting or twisting them off close to the plant base, but leave enough for the plant to survive. Keep a watch for slugs which can be a problem.

Thyme *(Thymus)*
Thyme can be grown from spring-sown seed, but seed tends to give inferior plants and it is best propagated by cuttings taken in late spring or autumn, or by root division.

Thyme needs full sun and perfect drainage so add sharp grit to the compost. Water regularly to establish the plants, but when they are growing well water only occasionally and don't add any fertiliser. Trim back after flowering to prevent the plants becoming straggly.

Tomato
(Lycopersicon esculentum)
Heavy-yielding tomatoes are excellent in large containers, and small-fruited varieties are ideal for patio pots and hanging baskets. The variety 'Tumbler' has been specially bred for growing in hanging baskets. Grow tomatoes from seed sown in warmth in spring and do not plant out until danger of frost has passed. One plant needs a 25–30cm (10–12in) pot. They must have full sun and wind protection. Position a stake in the pot before planting out young tomato plants. Water and feed regularly throughout the growing season with a high-potash liquid feed. Tie the plant in at intervals as it grows. You can pinch out the lateral shoots that develop at the base of the leaf stalks but this is not essential. You may also wish to cut out the growing tip once plants have developed well. Keep an eye out for pests such as whitefly. Small infestations can be dealt with by squeezing them between finger and thumb.

Turnips *(Brassica rapa)*
Turnips can be sown from late winter to September in deep containers. They should be thinned to 10cm (4in) apart. It is difficult to grow root vegetables in containers and they need a lot of care and attention if you are to get good results.

The plants need regular water and fertiliser in order to prevent roots from becoming coarse.

Watercress
(Nasturtium officinale)
It is possible to grow a delicious crop of watercress in a container. As the seedlings grow, stand the pot in a saucer of water. Do not let the water stagnate; completely change the water at least once a week. Keep cutting the stems to maintain growth. Watercress prefers a shady position.

Zucchini *(Cucurbita pepo)*
Zucchini, or courgettes, can be sown in warmth in spring and planted out after danger of frost has passed. There are smaller varieties suitable for container growing, but they will still need room to develop.

Plants need full sun or part shade and wind protection. Water regularly to maintain rapid growth. Once zucchini start to crop, the fruit enlarge rapidly, and you should check plants and pick daily. Powdery mildew and bacterial wilt can be a problem.

Lasting pleasures

Shrubs, trees and climbers

SHRUBS

However limited your space, do try to have at least one shrub to provide shape and background to your potted garden. Shrubs are perfect for container gardening as their rounded shapes can hide fences and decorate blank walls. They can be grown as a single specimen, with ground-cover or with an underplanting of annuals or bulbs for extra colour.

Try to choose a shrub that will give the most value over the longest period of time; many will offer colourful foliage and berries as well as the relatively brief display of flowers. Shrubs with fragrant flowers will double your gardening pleasure. While your shrubs are in flower, position them in a strategic spot – by the gate, at the front door, beside a path, on the patio or near a window, or even take them indoors for a short time.

Evergreens are invaluable for providing a year-round leafy background for seasonal plantings, and most are very decorative in their own right.

Small- to medium-sized shrubs are generally the easiest to grow in containers, but larger shrubs can be grown if you have the space and are willing to give them the extra care which many of them benefit from, such as annual topdressing or potting on. All shrubs will need regular pruning to maintain their size and shape, and, if possible, the container should be turned regularly to ensure even growth.

Fuchsias are classic container plants. Upright varieties are

An especially handsome container such as this sculptured urn deserves an equally choice plant like this dwarf, lavish blooming rose.

The bronze tints of cryptomeria sit well with curry plant, golden euonymus and winter heathers.

leaving about the top third of the foliage. Then move the plant to a large pot and tie the main stem to a stake. Position the stake close to the plant, but avoid damaging the roots. Lightly prune the top side branches to encourage rapid growth of the main trunk, and remove new shoots as they appear on the lower trunk. Regular, light feeding is required. When the desired height is reached, remove the growing tip. Pinch out the side branches to encourage an attractive bushy head. Always prune during the growing season as growth is more obvious and training easier then.

ROSES

A specialist rose grower will be able to give you the best advice on the right type of rose for container culture. Choose the best plants you can, as they will be seen at close quarters. Repeat-flowering varieties will give you a longer season of interest, and there are now many smaller modern patio roses and miniature roses that are more suited to growing in pots, troughs, urns and baskets. Many varieties can be trained as standards, and climbers and ramblers can be trained to cover

excellent in tubs and pots while cascading types are particularly well-suited to hanging baskets. Among many excellent shrubs to try are azaleas, cotoneasters, camellias, euonymus, hydrangeas, pyracanthas and viburnums.

Many shrubs can be trained as standards. Plants traditionally used for standards and topiary work are box, yew and bay tree, but flowering shrubs such as roses, fuchsias, marguerite daisies and even lavender can be trained into standards. Standard plants can be trained on a single stem, or weeping varieties can be grafted to the upright stem of another plant. Roses and weeping cherries can be grown this way.

Although standards can be bought, it is much cheaper and more fun to raise your own. Over three or four years train a plant with a bare stem to produce a rounded head of foliage and flowers. Look for single-stemmed, straight plants. Using very sharp secateurs, remove the lower branches on the central trunk,

Rhododendron 'Goldflimmer' is doubly valuable for its flowers and for its yellow splashed foliage.

Like most citrus, the dwarf calamondin orange grows well in pots.

walls and trellis, but avoid the most vigorous varieties.

As your roses get bigger, you must regularly move them into larger pots with fresh compost. This is best done in winter when they are dormant. If they are left in small pots they will soon become root bound and will dry out rapidly. Thorns can be a nuisance, and so avoid positioning large bushes close to walkways and doors. Roses need to be fed and watered regularly and must be grown in full sun.

TREES

Quite a number of decorative trees can be planted in containers. Trees add height and character to a potted arrangement and provide shade for people, pets and other plants.

Citrus trees are popular container plants for their shapely habit, scented blossom, aromatic evergreen foliage and edible fruit, but they need to be over-wintered in a greenhouse or conservatory.

They can form a useful windbreak and noise muffler, and can give a feeling of privacy to small city gardens.

Many trees stay quite small when they are confined to containers, but you should check the tree's ultimate potential size when making your selection. The container you choose for growing a tree should be sturdy and long lasting. As a young tree grows it will be necessary to repot it regularly in progressively larger containers.

Some of the Japanese maples are amongst the most popular trees for containers where, because the root spread is restricted, they grow more slowly. They are deciduous plants and will thrive in partial shade if they are kept well watered in dry times. For example, *Acer palmatum* 'Atropurpureum' has beautiful purple foliage, which changes to scarlet in autumn before falling.

FRUIT TREES

Fruit trees make delightful container specimens. Apart from bearing decorative fruit they will grace any potted garden with beautiful flowers and, in the case of citrus trees, a mass of handsome glossy leaves.

Buy your fruit trees from a specialist fruit grower, who will have a greater selection and may be able to advise you on the right varieties for containers and those suitable for your district. Some fruit trees, such as apples, pears and peaches, need to be grafted onto a dwarfing or other special rootstock. Normal varieties of fruit trees are too large to be grown in containers.

Always check whether the tree will need a mate for cross-pollination in order to bear fruit. For example, apples, pears and most plums need pollinators. A tree grafted with both the desired variety and the pollinator is ideal.

Use a loam-based John Innes type potting compost. Container-grown fruit trees require small applications of fertiliser throughout the growing season; a slow-release fertiliser is ideal.

Japanese maples will thrive in containers and give years of pleasure.

Even in containers you can team up a climber like this clematis with a sizeable shrub and see them in flower together.

Make sure newly planted trees do not suffer from moisture loss. You can prevent frost damage to spring fruit blossom by covering with a layer of horticultural fleece.

All citrus trees grow well in containers and their beautiful perfumed blossoms will be most appreciated near the house. They are, however, not hardy and should be grown in a sheltered, sunny position and brought into a cool greenhouse or conservatory, or sheltered porch during the winter.

CLIMBERS

In a small garden, or on a patio or balcony where space is at a premium, there are many advantages in using walls, fences and railings for growing rambling, trailing and climbing plants. Quite often the potential growing space on the walls is greater than the ground area.

Climbers can make any wall or screen look attractive and can provide you with privacy and shelter. They can be used to conceal ugly drain pipes, screen an unsightly view, soften bare walls or disguise the boundaries

of a balcony. A climber can become a feature in a tiny spot and can look as good tumbling from a specially raised urn as trained in a formal manner around a wire support or draped around a statue. One of the best things about climbers is that they provide colour or greenery at a higher level, an important consideration in a small area where many of the potted plants are at or very close to ground level.

Climbers can be grown successfully and effectively in containers if they are kept well fed, watered and trimmed. The restricted growing space may prevent vigorous types reaching their full extent, but this can be a benefit when the plants are positioned near the house and guttering. A restricted root-run will even encourage a profusion of flowers on some plants.

Most climbing plants need some type of support, such as wire mesh, trellis or poles, to help them climb and cover a wall effectively.

A support must be fixed firmly in place before the plants are positioned, since many will not make satisfactory progress unless

they have something to climb against from the start. Make sure that trelliswork is firmly fixed or it may be dislodged in strong winds. It is best to attach trellis or wires to wooden spacers fixed to the wall to allow air to circulate and the plant to weave in and out of the support.

Self-clinging climbers, such as ivy or Virginia creeper, may also need support as their suckers may disfigure walls if the vines need to be removed.

Choose a climber to suit your particular needs. Climbing roses, clematis, or the many annual climbers will give you lots of colourful flowers, while the ivies with variegated leaves will tolerate shade and bring life and charm to a dark corner. Some of the smaller-leaved ones can be tucked into hanging baskets where they make beautiful cascading plants.

Do not overlook fragrance when choosing a climbing plant for a pot. A sunny balcony wall or the side of a town house could be covered with an exquisitely scented jasmine, so that the delicious scent wafts in through the windows or doors when they are open during the summer.

Something different

Most gardeners are creative by nature and with
a little imagination can turn even the most unlikely spot
into a flourishing and fun garden. As well as the usual
pot plants, there are a number of less common gardening
techniques and plants you can use in a container garden.
You can create a varied and interesting display on a
much reduced scale – with bonsai trees or miniature
topiaries, or a compact miniature garden in a single pot
using undemanding succulents. Or try gardening without
soil by making a water garden.

*Left: This bonsai garden is centred on a fine 41-year-old red pine, a truly
magnificent example of the art.*

Bringing up bonsai

Bonsai is the old oriental art of dwarfing trees and growing them in small containers. The name is Japanese and, literally translated, means 'planted in a shallow container'.

From the beginning the tree is grown in a particular style and is shaped by pruning roots and branches, wiring and selective removal of growth.

Whether you begin by using seed, a cutting, a naturally stunted native plant or a mature container-grown plant, you will find bonsai a fascinating pastime that combines horticulture and art. If you give a bonsai plant regular care and attention, it will remain healthy and beautiful for very many years. Indeed, the best specimens can be several decades old.

Bonsai produced from seed can take many years to establish and it is easiest to start with two- or three-year-old plants that have been grown by specialist bonsai nurseries. These plants will usually have sufficient branches to show signs of character, so you can choose one suitable for the style of bonsai you want to grow, and training can be started immediately. They are chosen from species that adapt particularly well to dwarfing, including pine, cedar, spruce, privet, juniper, cotoneaster and azaleas. Deciduous trees such as ginkgo, hawthorn, crab apple, dogwood and maple are also used. As flowers are full-size, flowering bonsai can be quite spectacular.

Bonsai always look best displayed simply, as here, but you may prefer to replace or remove the nursery label.

BONSAI STYLES

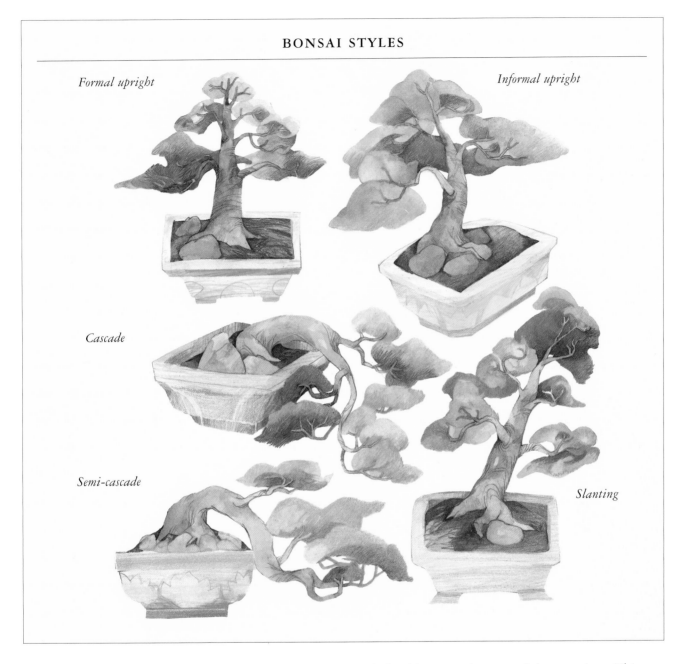

Formal upright

Informal upright

Cascade

Semi-cascade

Slanting

BONSAI STYLES

There are five basic styles of bonsai. Select the one that is best suited to your plant.

Formal upright
The shape is based on well-grown specimen trees. The trunk is vertical and tapers from bottom to top. The top is erect.

Informal upright
The trunk is slightly curved and the top bends slightly. Where the trunk curves, a branch on the outer side of the bend should curve away in the opposite direction.

Semi-cascade
The trunk grows straight up and then gently turns downward, with the tip of the tree reaching below the rim of the container. The trunk usually tilts up again at the tip.

Cascade
The trunk grows upwards, then turns downwards at a steep angle with the tip reaching below the bottom of the container. This style of bonsai is displayed on a high stand to prevent branch damage. Semi-cascade and full cascade bonsai are usually grown in a deep pot to give physical stability and to display the form to advantage.

Slanting
The trunk slants to either the right or left, with the lowest branch on the main trunk growing in the opposite direction to the slant to provide balance.

TRANSPLANTING BONSAI

If you are establishing a bonsai or repotting one, first prepare the container by covering the drainage holes with a piece of fine wire mesh to prevent soil loss. This is held in place by lengths of copper wire, which are threaded through one drainage hole, taken under the container and up through the other drainage hole. The excess wire will help hold the tree in place when it is potted. Cover the screen with a 1–2.5cm (0.5–1in) layer of specially formulated bonsai potting compost. Position the plant and add more potting mix, gently but firmly pushing the mix between the roots. Water to eliminate air pockets and fill spaces as necessary.

Most bonsai need repotting only every second year.

These 10-year-old Japanese maples have been dwarfed by growing in a small container

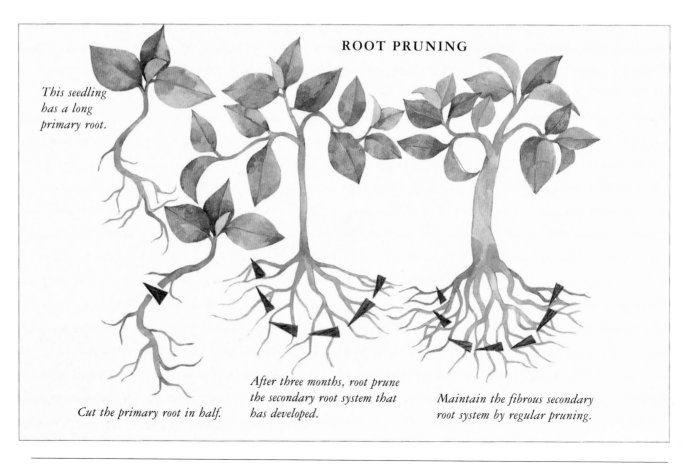

ROOT PRUNING

This seedling has a long primary root.

Cut the primary root in half.

After three months, root prune the secondary root system that has developed.

Maintain the fibrous secondary root system by regular pruning.

BRANCH PRUNING

A year-old seeding is pruned at the tip to encourage branching.

At two years a side branch is trained to become a new leader and the tips are pruned to encourage branching.

At three years the tips are again pruned, including the top one, to induce branching at the top of the plant.

ROOT PRUNING

Root pruning is necessary to maintain the health of the tree in a restricted environment. It is most important to prune the roots at the correct time. Root pruning is usually carried out in early spring when you first notice the swelling of leaf buds, before they burst open. Remove the bonsai and carefully loosen the potting mixture from the roots using a chopstick. Trim all the roots back to about a third of their original length.

Position the tree on the soil. Try placing it in a number of positions to see where it looks best. Take advantage of attractively shaped surface roots by making sure the tree is not too low in the container. Draw

A horizontally-trained fir growing in a soil-filled cleft in the rock.

the wires over the root mass and tie them together to steady the tree. Cut off excess wire. Fill in around the roots with potting mix so that no air spaces are left. A chopstick will help work soil in around the roots. Water the tree well with a fine spray. Place the bonsai plant in a shady spot for a couple of weeks, and then gradually allow it more light.

BRANCH PRUNING

Establish your basic line by branch pruning. Using sharp, small pruning tools, remove all minor branches that disguise the main lines. Try to arrange the branches so that the main lower branch goes either left or right, the second to the opposite side and the third to the back. Cut off twigs close to the trunk so that the cuts heal smoothly. Shorten long branches, especially those towards the tip of the tree.

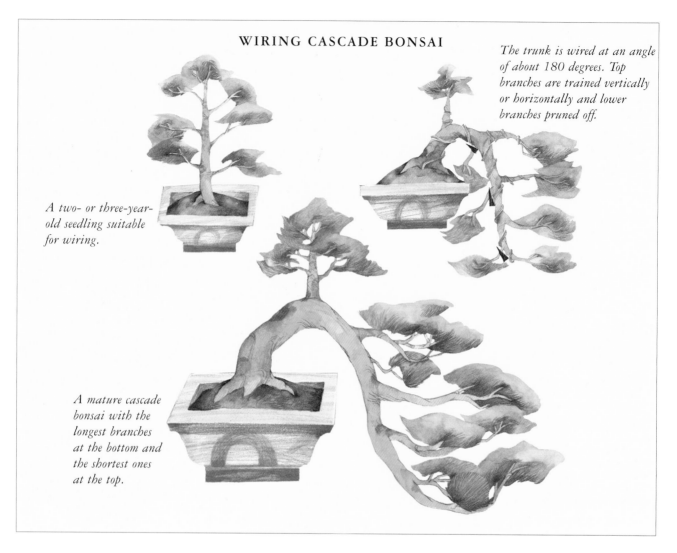

WIRING CASCADE BONSAI

The trunk is wired at an angle of about 180 degrees. Top branches are trained vertically or horizontally and lower branches pruned off.

A two- or three-year-old seedling suitable for wiring.

A mature cascade bonsai with the longest branches at the bottom and the shortest ones at the top.

WIRING

You may wish to shape the growth of the branches with copper wire. Starting at the base of the trunk, wind the wire around the trunk and branches, at the same time carefully bending the trunk, branches and twigs into position. Don't wire tightly, don't trap any leaves and don't force a branch too far in a new direction. After a month or two, when the plant has had a rest, you can adjust the wiring. After about six months the wires can be removed from small branches and from larger branches in a year or two. (If you receive a wired bonsai as a gift, you can remove the wire after similar periods.)

POSITIONING YOUR BONSAI

Do not take your outdoor bonsai indoors; they will do best when placed outside in a sunny or lightly shaded position that is protected from the wind. They will benefit from being rotated every week so that they receive even exposure to sunlight. In winter they need to be protected from severe frost.

Bonsai are best kept on tables or benches off the ground to avoid contact with pests and for ease of maintenance. The shelves should be slatted to allow good air circulation.

If you do need to take your bonsai indoors, return it outside as soon as possible.

WATERING

Your bonsai should never be allowed to dry out completely. In hot, dry, windy weather it may need watering two or three times a day. In winter, twice a week will usually be sufficient.

FEEDING

Be careful not to over-feed your bonsai and feed it only during the growing period, not during the winter season. A slow-release fertiliser can be used at the rate recommended by the manufacturer. Never apply fertiliser to dry soil: water the bonsai plant well first and then apply the fertiliser.

Cacti and other succulent plants

Succulents are fleshy plants that store moisture taken up during rainy periods to use later during periods of drought. They use ribs, spines, a waxy covering and the way they grow to maintain their air-cooling and water storage systems. Succulents include the cactus family, *Cactacae*, as well as several other plant families. There are two main types, stem succulents such as the cacti, and leaf succulents such as sempervivums, sedums and agaves.

True cactus plants generally have spines rising from special organs known as areoles. These are small cushion-like protruberances arranged regularly on the surface of the plant and generally each of them bears a number of spines. Only cacti have these areoles and so a cactus can easily be identified

*An old plant of hen and chicken (*Echeveria elegans*) here sprawls out of its tall, pedestalled container.*

The golden-spined Notocactus lenninghausii.

even when it has no spines at all.

Succulents come in a marvellous range of shapes, textures and flower types, and they look wonderful in all sorts of containers, especially shallow saucers and tubs in both formal and informal styles.

Their strong, spiky shapes look particularly good with many of the more modern garden designs and architecture, but they can blend in with almost any planting style.

Because they can stand up to dry, hot conditions they are often ideal for sunny, sheltered balconies and patios. They are the perfect container plants for any gardener who is away a lot of the time and is unable to water daily, as they can survive much longer periods without watering than most plants, and will still remain looking good. They are very adaptable and are extremely easy to grow, and insect pests and diseases don't seem to both them.

POTTING

It is best to grow cacti and other succulent plants in fairly small pots. If they are grown in large pots there is a chance that the soil will remain too wet for too long after watering and the roots may rot. When potting on, use a pot only one size larger. It is best to repot at the beginning of the growing period. As they are relatively slow-growing, most succulents will only need potting on about every three years, or when the plants become congested.

The container must have excellent drainage. A standard general-purpose potting compost is suitable for most succulents, but it should be mixed with one-third coarse sand, grit or perlite to improve the drainage. Special cactus composts are available at many nurseries and garden centres. A liquid feed should be given at approximately monthly

An upturned blue clay ridge tile makes a novel setting for drought-resistant succulents and Sedum *'Ruby Glow'.*

Fleshy-leaved alpines combined with pebbles, shells and a brick pot give this urn the flavour of the Mediterranean seabed.

intervals through the growing season, or, alternatively, a slow-release fertiliser can be used.

POSITIONING

Most plants from arid regions like to grow in an open, sunny position. However, plants growing in pots are susceptible to sun-scorching and may need protection from harsh afternoon sun in summer. They prefer a dry atmosphere and need good air circulation in humid conditions. They may also need shelter from rain if there is high summer rainfall. Some succulents can be grown outside all year round, but others are not very frost-tolerant and should be moved indoors for the winter. Some can be left outdoors if they are kept on the dry side and protected from hard or prolonged frosts.

WATERING

Succulents should be watered regularly during the growing season, but the compost should be allowed to almost dry out between waterings. Even during the main growing season in spring and summer, watering may be necessary only once a week. During winter, water should be given only about every four weeks.

Terracotta strawberry pots can be used to grow a collection of succulents.

Don't discard broken pots. They are ideal for drought-resistant succulents.

PROPAGATING

Cacti and other succulent plants can be propagated easily in moist, coarse sand in pots. Cuttings and detached pieces should be allowed to dry out for a day or two before they are inserted into the striking medium. If necessary, cuttings can be held in place by tying them to a small stake. Allow the sand to almost dry out before you water again.

EASY SUCCULENTS FOR CONTAINERS

Agave americana
The century plant is a half-hardy perennial growing to 90cm (3ft) or more which forms rosettes of grey-green, sword-shaped, sharp-toothed leaves. Grow in full sun and well-drained compost and propagate in early summer by offsets, which are freely produced. It rarely flowers in containers. Several variegated forms are available, with bold yellow or cream stripes on the leaves.

Echeveria
A genus of rosette-forming or bushy perennials with long-lasting flower spikes with many tubular flowers in summer. Plant them in groups in sun and very well drained soil and protect from hard frosts. Propagate by offsets, division or cuttings in summer.

Kalanchoe
Frost-tender, evergreen succulents, more often grown as houseplants, but which can be grown in garden containers through the summer. They have showy red, yellow or pink flowerheads. Grow in full sun or partial shade in well-drained soil and keep moist. Propagate by seed, offsets or stem cuttings in spring or summer.

Sedum
The stonecrops are succulents with either clump-forming or spreading habits. Flat heads of starry flowers are produced during the summer or early autumn. Grow in fertile, well-drained compost and water regularly during the growing season. Propagate by division in the spring, or cuttings in spring and summer.

Sempervivums
The houseleeks are fully hardy evergreen perennials which make ground-hugging mats of foliage. Clusters of flowers, held well above the dense rosettes of narrow leaves, are produced in summer. Rosettes die after flowering, but leave numerous offsets. Remove stems immediately the flowers fade. Plant in groups in gritty compost. They prefer sun but will tolerate light shade, and will grow more strongly if watered regularly. Propagate by offsets in summer.

WATER GARDENS IN CONTAINERS

These Chinese containers were originally intended for goldfish.

What would a water garden be without water lilies? Small varieties such as 'Alba' and 'Helvola' are ideal for container culture.

A glazed pot without drainage holes is quite unsuitable for conventional planting but will make a wonderful small water garden, as will other containers, such as a wooden half-barrel or even plastic tubs. Stocked with a few water lilies or water hawthorn and a couple of fish, a pot can provide an effective point of interest in small gardens.

Position the pot in a sunny spot away from trees, which may drop their flowers and leaves and pollute the water. Don't worry about the pond being near windows or doors: the fish prevent mosquitoes becoming a problem.

Place the pot in position before filling with water and planting. The easiest way to plant is to use the plastic baskets designed for use in ponds. Line the basket with a square of hessian, fill with aquatic compost, position the plant and cover the compost with gravel to prevent it floating away. Different types of plants will need to be positioned at different levels in the tub. Stand pots of marginal plants, such as *Iris kaempferi*, on bricks to bring them closer to the surface.

Early to mid spring is the best time to plant water lilies. Position the lilies and slowly fill the pot with water. It doesn't matter if your lilies are a little short and are submerged. Within a few days the leaf stalks will stretch up to the sun and settle on top of the water. A number of beautiful miniature water lilies, including varieties of *Nymphaea pygmaea*, are fine for containers.

If you want to introduce fish to your pond you will need some oxygenating aquatic plants to help absorb impurities and keep the water clean. You may also want to introduce some floating plants. If you choose duckweed or fairy moss (*Azolla*) be prepared to scoop it out regularly or it will cover the surface. Avoid floating pondweed, which is too rampant and will also quickly cover the surface, cutting off oxygen. A successful pond has the surface partially clear of plants to allow the sun to get to the water, but enough foliage for oxygenation and to allow the fish to hide from birds. Remove any dead water lily leaves to prevent them polluting the water. As the pond is so small, it must be kept clean. Introduce a couple of water snails to each tub; they help to keep the water clean by eating decaying vegetation.

Potting essentials

If you are new to gardening or have limited time, you can still have

success with potted plants; the trick is to begin with only a few pots.

Just follow a few simple rules:

match the scale of the plant to the container, select a suitable potting

mix, make sure the growing conditions are right,

position the plants for maximum effect and you have provided the

essential requirements for a successful container garden.

CHOOSING A CONTAINER

Choosing the right container for your garden can be just as important as choosing the plants to go in it. While the choice will always depend on your own personal style, the effect you are trying to create and your budget, the container should be an appropriate design for its intended position and should be of a style and shape to show off the plants to best advantage.

Practical considerations, such as size, depth, weight and cost, will inevitably also influence your choice, but an exciting and increasing variety of pots is now available for all budgets and you should have no problem finding a selection to suit whatever style you choose for your garden.

When considering the size of container to use, you will find that smaller pots are more versatile and are much easier to move around, but larger pots can contain a bigger display and will need watering less frequently. A low container will focus attention on the plants, while a large decorative pot can be as much a part of the display as the plants it contains.

The position a pot is to occupy must affect the choice of shape and style, whether you want it to blend in with its surroundings or stand out as an eye-catching focal point, but personal taste is perhaps the ultimate deciding factor. While some prefer elegant, simple lines, others prefer elaborate and ornate decoration.

You can completely change the character of a display by your choice of container style. Ornate urns or 'Versailles tubs', for example, are more suited to a formal garden, while simple terracotta pots or wicker baskets will instantly conjure up a cottage garden feel, and brightly coloured pots in unusual shapes or materials will create a more modernistic effect.

Whichever style of container you choose, bear in mind that it is easy to knock or brush against pots on a small patio, so avoid any containers with sharp or rough edges, and make sure that they are securely positioned.

MATCHING CONTAINERS AND PLANTS

When choosing containers for a particular display, select sizes and shapes of pot to suit the scale of your plants and the position you have chosen for them. Don't put a tree in a small pot that will topple over in the slightest breeze, or low-growing plants in a tall pot where they will seem small and lost.

Plants grown in containers that are too small quickly fill the pot with their roots and exhaust the soil. Small pots dry out very quickly in hot weather and are difficult to maintain. On the other hand, if you place a small plant in a large pot, the potting mix could remain damp in the middle for too long and cause root problems. Shrubs and small trees will need a deep tub to accommodate their large roots, while flowers and bulbs look good and are most comfortable in a wide, saucer-shaped dish.

As well as shape and size, consider the colour and texture of the container and whether it will blend with your chosen plants. Natural colours and textures, such as wood, stone or terracotta, will complement the plants and help create a restful effect, while bright colours and unusual materials and textures will add vibrancy and impact. Bold containers lend themselves to bold planting styles, with architectural plants or brilliant colour schemes.

Some plants look better in certain types of container. For example, rockery plants will look more at home in a stone trough than in an ornate urn. Trailing plants will need somewhere to trail to make the most of their effect, so do not put them in a low container. It would also be a waste to grow them in a highly

The blue-grey colour of this trio of pots is reflected in the planting.

decorated container as this would soon become completely hidden by the trailing growth. However, trailing plants will disguise an ugly container. They are also useful for linking the display in a group of containers of different heights, and to soften the rigid lines of steps and entrance ways.

DO IT YOURSELF

If, despite the great choice available, you can't find just the right container, it is not difficult to make your own. Two major advantages are that you can make something that is exactly the right size to fit a particular space, such as a narrow windowsill or awkward corner of the patio, and that you can create something that is totally original.

It is also possible, of course, to give any commercially produced pot an original treatment by decorating it yourself. There are paints available that will cover most materials, and stencilled or freehand decoration will add a personal touch to what was a standard mass-produced pot. Consult any good craft book for tips on paints and techniques.

Set the theme by choosing an oriental pot for your Japanese maple.

IMPROVISING CONTAINERS

Anything that can hold compost can be used to grow plants, as long as holes can be made for drainage and the material is inert and does not react with fertilisers, moisture or chemicals. Old wheelbarrows and bathtubs are now quite widely used, and while they may have become a bit of a cliche, they can still make a spectacular display in the appropriate setting. These days, however, anything goes and everything from a pair of old wellies to a toilet has been used as a container for plants. With a little inventiveness, you will find that there are lots of simple things that can easily be found about the house and garden and used to grow plants. Try, for example, old watering cans and buckets, assorted tin cans, beer crates, logs, barrels, chamber pots, coal scuttles, kettles – just use your imagination.

MATERIALS

Wood
Wood is a versatile, natural material making an ideal

background for plants, and timber containers are always popular and blend easily with most settings. Wood lends itself equally well to formal designs, such as Versailles tubs, and informal designs, such as rustic half-barrels. Ready-made boxes are available in a wide variety of designs, and, being easy to cut and assemble, wood is also ideal for making containers to your own original design. If not already pre-treated, wooden boxes should be treated with a preservative that does not harm plants; never use creosote. To prolong the life of wooden boxes, a plastic liner can be used to grow the plants in. Wood is medium weight and can be used for quite large containers, and is a good insulator, evening out extremes of temperature. It is also easy to paint to match – or contrast with – its surroundings, or complement a planting scheme.

Stone

Stone can make a very attractive setting for plants, but as well as being expensive it is very heavy. This means it is only suitable for ground level containers, and it should be positioned carefully before planting, as a stone container is not easy to move. The colour and texture will depend on the type of stone used, but they all rapidly acquire an attractive, weathered appearance, and are long-lasting and maintenance-free.

Reconstituted stone or concrete are much cheaper alternatives and are available moulded into a wide variety of decorative shapes. They too are heavy, strong and long-lasting, making them suitable for large, permanent plantings. While they can look a bit stark when new, they can be 'aged' by painting some live yogurt on the outside to encourage the growth of lichens and mosses.

A rusty firebasket is an inspired choice for a spring show of fiery tulips.

Metal

Lead, copper or iron containers are now rarely seen because of their high cost and the problems of rust and corrosion, although it is still possible to find very decorative antique containers at auction. Although expensive and heavy, they are long-lasting and attractive, especially those that have acquired the patina of age.

Terracotta

Terracotta has long been one of the most popular materials for garden pots, and is available in lots of sizes and styles, from the simple to the ornate. Its rich red-brown earthy appearance sets off most plants very well, and it weathers to an attractive, natural finish. Terracotta is a porous material and unglazed pots will dry out rapidly and so need to be watered more often. They are also more difficult to clean and disinfect before replanting.

Most terracotta pots are relatively cheap, although the more elaborate or handmade pots can be quite expensive, but they are quite brittle and need to be handled carefully to avoid damage. If you want to leave your containers out over winter, check that they are frost-proof, as some, particularly those imported from Mediterranean countries, are not, and will crack or flake if exposed to frosty conditions.

Glazed terracotta pots, available in a range of decorative finishes, retain moisture better and are easier to clean and disinfect. Glazed and unglazed stoneware also retains moisture better and is frost-proof.

Plastic

Plastic containers are cheap, light in weight and retain moisture well. Their disadvantage is that they have tended to discolour and deteriorate very quickly and were not as stylish in appearance as many of the other materials available. However, many of the modern plastics are much more durable, and in recent years a wide range of much more effective designs have become available, including those that have the appearance of other materials, such as terracotta.

Plastic pots now come in many different shapes and sizes, ranging from large tubs suitable for small trees to bulb bowls. Being lightweight they are relatively easy to move and ideal for balconies. If you are using a lot of plastic pots, you will achieve a more harmonious effect by sticking to one colour: black is a good neutral colour, fading into the background, but plastic pots are now available in a much wider range of colours.

Fibreglass

Fibreglass has been used to simulate natural materials, giving a cheap, lightweight and long-lasting alternative to materials such as stone. It is safe for plants and frostproof, but can be brittle.

Good culture and care

POTTING COMPOSTS

To produce a really stunning display, containers must be filled with a good potting mixture. Give them a poor compost and the plants will soon show you that they are unhappy.

Never use soil from the garden as this is likely to be too heavy, drain poorly and will contain weed seeds. A good commercial potting mix is made from clean, weed-free components and will contain sufficient nutrients for balanced plant growth over some weeks or months. There are two main types of potting compost; loam or soil-based mixes, such as John Innes, and soil-less types.

John Innes potting composts can be made at home, but most people prefer to buy them ready-mixed. They contain sterilised loam, peat and sand in prescribed proportions, plus a balanced fertiliser mixture. Soil-based mixes are generally better for larger specimens and for long-term planting.

Soil-less composts can also be mixed at home or purchased ready mixed. Traditionally they contain peat blended with sharp sand and a slow-release fertiliser, but mixes containing peat substitutes such as coconut fibre (coir) or shredded bark are becoming more widely available. Soil-less composts are lighter and easier to handle, but can be harder to re-wet if they dry out, and the plants rapidly use up the nutrients in them so regular feeding soon becomes necessary.

Different plants prefer different potting mixes. At your local nursery, garden centre or diy store you will find a variety of ready-made mixes tailored to individual plant needs, such as bulb mix, orchid compost and camellia and azalea mixes, as well as specific mixes suitable for hanging baskets and seed raising. These mixes will contain the correct humus proportions and necessary nutrients to get the plants off to a good start.

If you mix your own compost you can also vary the mix to suit the needs of individual plant groups. For example, you might want to increase the quantity of moisture-holding peat for ferns, hanging baskets and window-boxes, or add more coarse sand to improve the drainage for your sun-loving plants.

Old, used compost may harbour pests and diseases and nutrients are likely to be exhausted, so always use new compost when planting up, or if you are replanting a pot, replace at least the top half of the old compost with new material.

DRAINAGE

Roots will rot if drainage is poor and the compost becomes waterlogged. All containers should have good-sized drainage holes in the base for water to escape easily. Before filling pots with compost, cover the bottom with drainage material such as crocks, stones or gravel. The important thing is that drainage holes should always be kept clear of any obstruction and not blocked by caked potting material.

It is also important for the welfare of both pots and plants that the water drains quickly away from the ground on which the pots are standing. Placing containers clear of the ground on stands or bricks allows excess water to run off freely. It also helps to minimise the chances of harbouring slugs and snails. Never leave pots standing in saucers even partly filled with water. This causes waterlogging and is fatal to many plants, especially during the winter months.

WATERING

As a general guide the soil in a container should not be allowed to dry out completely before you water. Look for early signs of wilting and test for moisture by feeling the compost with your fingers or testing the weight of the pot. In hot, dry and windy conditions you will need to check each container daily. If the top few centimetres are dry or the pot feels very light, you will need to water. Be sure to completely soak the compost. Remember that even if the top layer of compost is wet it may still be very dry underneath, especially if peat-based compost is used.

The frequency of watering will depend upon a variety of factors, including the weather, the air temperature, the size of the pot and the type of plant (for example, ferns like to be slightly moist at all times while plants such as lavender and rosemary prefer to dry out between waterings). The drier and hotter it is the more water your plants will need – watering twice a day may be necessary for very small pots during the summer months. It helps to minimise evaporation if the plants are given protection from hot afternoon sun. A mulch of shredded bark or gravel will also help conserve moisture and keep down weeds.

Watering is best done in the early morning or late afternoon, so that evaporation is at a minimum and the plants have some hours to absorb the water. If plants are drooping in the middle of the day during a heat wave, feel the compost. If it is moist the wilting is just a protective mechanism and the plants will pick up after the sun has gone off them. If the mix is dry, then water at the base of the plant. If you splash water onto the foliage in bright sunshine it may scorch.

In general, water containers using a can with a fine rose or with a hose nozzle that gives a gentle spray, not a jet of water. Alternatively, you can use a trickling hose and move it from tub to tub after each plant has had a long, steady soak. A hose with a lance attachment is very useful for reaching hanging baskets or pots at the back of a display. 'Self-watering' containers have a reservoir of water which the plants can draw on as they need to, and therefore you will not need to water them quite as frequently.

If you have a lot of containers or hanging baskets, watering can be very time consuming and you may find it is worth installing an automatic watering system with a system of pipes attached to an outdoor tap, with branches fitted with drippers going to each pot or hanging basket. Sophisticated timing devices can also be connected to outdoor taps to control the times of watering.

Such systems can be particularly valuable when you are on holiday.

Remember that rain will not necessarily reach all outdoor container plants, especially those protected by overhanging eaves or verandahs. Also, dry windy weather in winter can quickly deplete your pots of moisture. Don't forget to check the reservoirs of self-watering containers to ensure they are topped up.

If a container or hanging basket has really dried out, stand it in a bucket or a bath of water overnight to re-wet the rootball.

Containers of all kinds will need less water in winter and it is important not to overwater them or the roots may rot and the plants will die. On the other hand, do not neglect them, they will still need some water.

It is a good idea to mix some water-retaining granules with the compost before planting your containers, as these will increase the water-holding capacity of the compost so that you will need to water less frequently. This can be particularly valuable for hanging baskets that dry out very rapidly.

FEEDING

Plants growing in containers will inevitably require more frequent and more careful feeding than those growing in the open ground because of the limited nutrients in the compost, particularly in small containers. The more plants there are in a container, the more rapidly they will exhaust the nutrients.

During the first few weeks plants growing in good potting mixtures usually do not need feeding. After that plants will gradually exhaust the food supply. Nutrients are also quickly leached away by rain and constant watering.

Fertilisers should only be given when the plants are in active growth, which is usually from spring to early autumn. Never apply fertiliser to dry soil or potting mix – water the plants first, apply the fertiliser and then water again.

There are various ways of applying fertiliser. Solid or dry fertilisers, sold as granules or powders, can be mixed with the compost before planting or applied as a top dressing, depending on their type.

Liquid feeds are an easy way of feeding a lot of container plants. They are simply diluted according to the manufacturer's instructions and watered on from a watering can, or sprayed through a special hose attachment.

Perhaps simplest of all are the pellets or sticks of slow-release fertilisers that can be put into the compost and which will release their fertiliser over a long period of time, often up to six months, removing the need for regular weekly or fortnightly feeds.

High potash feeds are best for flowers, and high nitrogen feeds for foliage, but for mixed plantings a general purpose balanced fertiliser is usually the best. If you find your container plants are showing signs of trace element or mineral deficiency, the quickest way to correct this is with a foliar feed, which is taken up very quickly by the plants. And compost itself is an excellent food and if used regularly to top up large containers will improve soil texture as well as providing necessary nutrients.

Planting

The first thing to do is to plan your display and select your plants. You will need to give some thought to how the plants will be positioned in the container, and if you are not certain of the effect, try out different combinations and arrangements of the plants before taking them out of their existing pots. Consider plant heights and colours and type of growth, and whether the container will be seen from one side or whether it will be a central feature viewed from all directions.

Make sure the plants you choose are compact and healthy with plenty of flowerbuds, and free from all signs of pests and disease. Avoid starved plants with pale green or yellowing leaves or those that have been heavily cut back. It is also best to reject plants that have been allowed to dry out and are shedding leaves or wilting. It is

tempting to purchase bedding plants that are already in flower as these will give an immediate effect, but they can sometimes be root-bound or starved, so do check them carefully before you buy.

Many plants used for summer container displays are only half hardy and can be damaged by frosts. Bear this in mind when planning your containers and do not put them outside too early. If you have a coldframe or green-house, however, you can plant up a half hardy arrangement early, keeping it under cover, and have a well-established display in full bloom ready to put out as soon as all danger of frost has passed.

Give all the plants a thorough watering about an hour before planting. Make sure that the container you are using is thoroughly clean, and is firmly positioned on a level base. Small containers can be planted up, either in their final positions or

in a greenhouse or conservatory and moved into position once they come into flower. However, if you are using a large container it is best to put it in its final position before planting as it will be too heavy for you to move it around easily once it is full.

Alternatively, it is possible to plant up a plastic flowerpot which can be placed inside a larger decorative container once the plants start to flower.

Good drainage is essential to avoid waterlogged conditions which will cause the plant to rot. Make sure there are adequate drainage holes in the base of the pot, and place a layer of polystyrene chunks or stones over the holes. The pot should be raised up from the ground so that water can drain away. You can save on the amount of compost needed for larger pots by putting an extra layer of drainage material in the base or by adding a layer of inert,

Remove any excess roots beneath the pots so the plants slide out easily.

Get your centrepiece in position first, in this case a purple cordyline.

Fill in with seasonal plants, adding more compost between the root balls.

lightweight material such as polystyrene chips.

Part fill the container with compost, gently firming it down. For a memorable display it is important to use only good quality compost. Water retentive-granules and slow-release fertiliser can be added to the compost to reduce the amount of watering and feeding the container plants will need. If you are using plants that require support, position the stake or trellis before putting the plants in.

Start planting at the centre or back of the container, positioning the plants with the deepest root balls first. Take your plant and support the stem between the fingers of one hand and turn the pot upside down. If the root ball does not readily slip out, hold the pot the right way up and tap the side of the pot, before again turning it upside down.

Gently spread out the roots and set the plant in the new container at the same depth as before. Cover the roots with compost and firm the soil down gently to avoid any air pockets around the roots. Plants at the

The finished pot gives rich contrasts of foliage and flowers.

edge of the container can be angled slightly to encourage them to drape over the sides of the container.

Try to keep compost off the leaves and flowers when planting as this can be difficult to clean off, particularly from plants with hairy leaves. Fill the container with compost to about an inch from the top, leaving room for watering, and firm down well. Water thoroughly.

In most cases the container can be left as it is as the plants will soon cover the compost entirely, but for trees and shrubs, or any situation where the surface will show, it is a good idea to cover the compost with a layer of mulch such as shredded bark or gravel. This not only improves the appearance but will also help retain moisture and prevent hardening of the soil. Additionally, it will protect the roots from heat in summer.

In general, plants need to be planted to the same depth they were in their original pots. Most bulbs need to be planted below the surface of the compost, to the correct depth for each type of bulb, and in a mixed container display should generally be put in before the other plants.

When planting a container of bulbs only, the bulbs can be planted in a double layer to give twice the number of flowers for a more impressive show. If they are positioned carefully, the bulbs in the lower layer will grow up between those in the upper layer, even when they are quite closely planted.

When potting up perennials, shrubs and trees, don't be tempted to put a small plant into a large pot. Small plants in large containers may suffer from root rot and die. Additionally, putting a flowering or fruiting shrub or tree in too large a container

When planting a tree or shrub, tease out some of the roots first so it grows away quickly into the new compost.

stimulates excess root growth at the expense of flowers and fruit.

As a plant grows it should be potted on and as a general rule the new pot should be about 5cm (2in) wider and deeper than the previous one.

When planting a display of summer bedding, make sure that you fill the container well and do not skimp on the number of plants if you want to ensure a good display. The secret here is to pack in as many plants as possible. Salad crops and vegetables need different treatment, however, as they need plenty of room to grow and develop a good crop.

Temporary planting can be added to a larger container which already has some established plants by setting smaller pots of plants inside the main container. This allows you to add a variety of seasonal plants, such as spring-flowering bulbs, summer bedding or winter-flowering heathers, and to change them around without disturbing the established permanent planting.

Increasing your stock

You can buy established plants for your container garden from any nursery or garden centre, but it is cheaper and more satisfying to grow your own. You will need some seed-raising compost, hormone rooting powder or liquid, good quality potting mix and some pots or seed trays. If you are reusing old containers, scrub them clean with a brush and a little detergent and rinse well before potting. Apart from making them look fresh, this will also remove any disease pathogens.

It is easy to increase your stock of favourite plants by taking cuttings. Pelargoniums such as this 'Pink Capricorn' can be propagated by softwood cuttings.

SEED

Growing plants from seed is easy and is the method used for annuals, vegetables, many herbs and some perennials.

Seeds can be sown in pots, trays or in their permanent container. You can purchase a commercial seed-raising compost or make your own using three parts coarse washed sand to one part peat moss or a substitute such as coconut fibre (coir). Do not put any fertiliser into the mix.

Sow the seed as evenly as possible and cover it with the seed-raising mix or sand. Very fine seed can be mixed with dry sand to make sowing easier and more even, while seeds that are large enough to handle can be well spaced and planted where they are to grow. A general rule in seed sowing is to plant seed at a depth of twice the diameter of the seed. Very fine seed such as lobelia and begonia should be barely covered while large seeds such as beans, sweet peas and nasturtium should be planted about 2.5cm (1in) deep. Check the instructions on the packet for

the best results. Lightly firm the surface of the compost with your hand or a flat piece of wood. Water gently so as not to dislodge the seed, or sit the container in shallow water and allow the water to soak up from the base (but do not leave the container sitting in water). Seed containers should be placed in a warm spot and watered often enough to keep them moist but not soggy.

Once the seed has germinated, keep the compost moist but not overwet or the tiny seedlings will rot. Seedlings should be transplanted as soon as they are large enough to handle. They can be potted individually or in groups, using a good quality potting mix. Place the plants in a sheltered, light spot until they are well established. Keep the compost moist, grow on and harden off until they are ready to be planted out into their permanent positions.

In containers flowers can be planted much closer than they

would be in the garden, as the containers look so much better when full of plants. Vegetables, however, should be well spaced to allow for optimum growth.

DIVISION

Divide clumps of perennials in late autumn or in late winter, before they start to make fresh growth. Lift the plant from its pot or bed and shake off excessive soil. Spread the roots gently apart and break or cut the clump to separate the young healthy sections from any dead old wood. Cut off any torn or damaged roots cleanly with secateurs or a sharp knife.

Select healthy sections with good roots and pot each new plant in a clean pot. Water it in well and place it in a shady spot for a few days to recover. Plants suitable for division include agapanthus, daylily, arum lily, lamb's ear, ajuga, pinks, chrysanthemum, campanula, hosta, helleborus and chives.

TAKING SEMI-RIPE CUTTINGS

Cut off tip (about 10cm (4in) long) above a leaf joint and remove lower leaves.

Insert cuttings around edges of pot and firm soil.

Create a moist atmosphere by erecting a wire frame over the pot and covering it with a polythene bag.

Water the cuttings.

Some plants with a fibrous root system, such as perennial phlox, thyme and oregano, need not be lifted. Choose a new shoot of young growth with roots already attached and use a sharp knife to cut it from the base of the plant.

STEM CUTTINGS

Taking cuttings is an easy and cheap method of propagation and provides a sure way of getting a plant exactly like the parent. A stem cutting is a small piece of stem taken from a healthy plant. It grows roots when inserted into a suitable cutting medium.

You can buy ready-made propagating mix or make your own from equal parts coarse sand, peat or peat substitute and perlite. A hormone rooting powder or liquid is not essential but it helps speed up the rooting process.

There are three main types of stem cuttings: softwood cuttings, semi-ripe cuttings and hardwood cuttings.

Softwood cuttings

These tip cuttings are taken in spring from the fast-growing tips of plants. Make sure the tips are reasonably firm and the lower

Choose healthy, non-flowering shoots for use as softwood cuttings.

Make a clean cut immediately below a leaf joint and trim off the lower leaves.

Insert the cuttings around the edge of a pot. Plastic drinks bottles make useful mini-greenhouses to prevent water loss.

leaves are fully developed. Suitable plants include pelargoniums, chrysanthemums, marguerites, fuchsias, lavender and rosemary.

Semi-ripe cuttings are taken from mid to late summer when the tip of the stem is leafy and firm but the base is hardening and becoming woody. Suitable plants include azaleas, camellias, daphne, hydrangea, lavender and santolina.

Hardwood cuttings are taken from the dormant wood of deciduous shrubs and trees. Taken in late autumn or winter after leaf fall, these cuttings are sturdy but slow to root. Suitable plants include honeysuckle, hydrangea, roses and deciduous viburnums.

Semi-ripe cuttings

To take a semi-ripe cutting, select a healthy growing tip about 10–15cm (4–6in) long and cut it off immediately below a leaf joint with a sharp knife. Trim the base and carefully remove the leaves from the lower third of the stem, so that no leaves will rest on the compost when it is planted. Dip

the base of the cutting into the rooting hormone.

Fill a pot with a commercial cutting compost and moisten. Use a clean stick or chopstick to make a hole in the compost about half the depth of the cutting. Put the cutting in the hole so that its end rests firmly on the bottom. Insert three or four cuttings around the edge of the pot. Push the mix around the cuttings and water gently but well to settle the mix and cutting (see the diagrams on page 87).

Create a moist greenhouse atmosphere for the pot by covering it with a plastic bag, which should be supported on a wire arch or small stakes to keep it from touching the cuttings. Secure the bag over the pot with an elastic band. The pot should be kept in a warm, light place, but out of direct sunlight. Keep the mix moist but not wet. Once new leaves appear the cuttings will be ready to be transferred to their individual pots. Place the newly potted plants in a protected, light spot for a couple of weeks before exposing them to more sunlight.

Hardwood cuttings

Many shrubs can be propagated from hardwood cuttings taken in autumn and overwintered in a coldframe or in a sheltered part of the garden.

Cut pieces of a healthy stem of this year's growth, about 6mm (0.25in) thick and 20–25cm (8–10in) long, cutting just above a bud. Trim off any sideshoots and remove the lower leaves of cuttings taken from evergreen plants.

To encourage rooting, wound each cutting at the base by removing the outer wood with a sharp knife. Insert the cuttings around the edge of a pot of gritty compost, so that up to two-thirds of their length is buried. Firm, water, label and place in a coldframe.

Alternatively, insert the cuttings in a trench in sheltered part of the garden.

Hardwood cuttings can take several months to root, but they should be well-rooted by the following autumn, when they can be repotted into individual pots or planted out in the garden.

Seedlings can be transferred to cell trays to make larger plants for display pots

Split up crowns of hostas in April, using a sharp knife.

Cuttings in water

Plants, such as ivy, busy lizzie (*Impatiens*) and fuchsias, will send out roots if their stalks are placed in water.

Make sure that the leaves do not touch the water. You can make a support by stretching some plastic cling wrap over a jar and poking the cuttings through it into the water. Water roots are more delicate than ordinary roots, so take care when transplanting the cuttings.

LAYERING CLIMBERS

Climbers such as clematis, honeysuckle, ivy and wisteria, can be propagated by layering from summer to autumn.

Prepare a pot with a gritty potting compost. Untie a healthy, vigorous, non-flowering shoot that is long enough to be anchored down. Gently bend the stem down, and with a sharp knife make an angled cut in the underside of the stem, close to a node. Hormone rooting powder can be applied to the wound, though vigorous climbers such as wisteria are unlikely to need it.

Peg the stem firmly into the compost using one or more U-shaped pieces of wire, cover with compost and keep moist.

Once the layer has rooted, sever it from the parent plant and grow it on, watering and feeding with a liquid fertiliser regularly, and repotting it as required.

RUNNERS

Some plants, such as strawberries, send out runners that develop small plants. Peg the tip of the runner into the soil or a pot of compost. Once they have taken root, they can be carefully cut from the parent and repotted.

Tradescantias are valuable trailers and root very easily from cuttings.

Trim off lower leaves of cuttings 8-10cm (3-4in) long and insert in pots of compost.

Looking after your containers

ROUTINE CARE

Neglect will rapidly result in weak and unattractive plants which are susceptible to pests and disease, but a little regular routine care will keep your container plants healthy and looking their best.

It almost goes without saying that it is essential that all plants are watered and fed regularly as they are in the restricted environment of the container (see pages 82–3).

Good hygiene is also important, and all debris and weeds should be promptly removed as should any dying foliage and dead flowers, or they could provide a breeding ground for all sorts of pests and diseases.

Deadheading also encourages a longer season of flowering, and in some bedding plants it can also improve the quality of the blooms.

Some plants benefit from harder cutting back than just deadheading. For example, if pelargoniums are cut back hard by a third or more after flowering this will produce a further flush of new growth and more flowers.

Many container plants benefit from regular pruning and training. Pinching out the growing tips of fuchsias, for example, will encourage a neat bushy habit, although many of the new bedding plants available now such as geraniums are bred to be compact and to branch freely.

Topiary and trained shrubs and climbers will need regular trimming throughout the growing season to keep them looking smart.

When pruning plants in a mixed planting look not only at the individual plants but also at the overall shape of the display and remove any shoots that are spoiling the appearance.

Sometimes you may need to remove plants that are not growing well, or indeed those that are perhaps growing too well and creating an imbalanced or lop-sided display.

Plants that have finished flowering before the others can also be removed and replaced with new plants that will continue the show.

Check climbers and tall-growing plants that need support regularly, making sure that they are securely tied in as they grow to keep them looking their best and so that they will not be damaged by flopping under their own weight, or by strong winds and heavy rains.

Long-term plantings, such as trees and shrubs will benefit from having the top few inches of compost removed and replaced with fresh material at least once during the growing season.

POTTING ON & REPOTTING

Plants that have outgrown their containers or look in need of rejuvenation should be potted on, and this is best carried out during cool weather either in the late winter or the early spring.

If roots have grown through the drainage holes, trim them off before trying to remove the plant from the pot.

First, ease the plant out of the pot and loosen the rootball. Carefully remove as much of the old soil as possible and gently loosen closely matted roots. Cut back any dead, damaged or diseased roots with clean, very sharp secateurs.

The top of the plant may also be lightly pruned back if you have removed a great many of the roots.

Position the plant in a larger pot, about 5cm (2in) wider than the original, or, if you want, repot a plant that has been root pruned back into its original container.

The container should have been thoroughly cleaned and filled with fresh potting mix so the plant is at the same level as it was originally. Top up the container with potting mix and water the plant gently but well.

If possible, place the newly potted plant in a protected position out of direct sunlight for a few days, and don't forget to water it regularly.

SEASONAL CARE

In hot weather, plants may need protection from the sun and should be moved into the shade. It is essential to check watering requirements at least once a day. Spraying leaves in the morning, before the sun gets too strong, may help overcome wilting. Spraying in the evening may help to replace moisture lost, but it is not a good idea to leave plants overnight with a lot of moisture on their leaves as this can encourage fungus diseases.

If you are going away on holiday move your containers to sheltered, shaded areas, and try to arrange for someone to water them regularly. Alternatively, stand them on capillary matting that is kept damp from a reservoir of water such as a bucket or trough.

Short-term summer displays can be pulled up and disposed of at the end of the season, but long-term or winter displays may need some protection during the coldest spells.

If you cannot bring your containers into the greenhouse or other sheltered area, it is certainly a good idea to take some precautions to protect both plants and containers from frost damage. Many modern containers on sale at garden centres and shops are frost-proof, but by no means all of them are, so it is always wise to check before you buy.

Containers that you know are definitely not frost-proof should be emptied and stored somewhere dry and frost-free until the spring.

Damp will increase the risk of frost damage, so make sure that your pots have good drainage and keep them on the dry side over winter.

This will also reduce the possibility of waterlogging which is one of the major reasons for the loss of container plants during the winter. Bulbs, for example, are particularly prone to rotting.

Plants should be given a thick mulch, such as bark chippings, and the leaves of spreading plants can be loosely tied together for extra protection.

Group pots together, and if possible give them additional protection by keeping them close to the warmth and shelter of the house or other building.

In the past plant pots were wrapped in layers of straw or bracken for extra protection, and this can still be used, although plastic bubble wrap makes a simple and effective modern substitute and is easier to handle.

Plants in small pots are especially vulnerable and should either be taken into a more sheltered area, plunged into a bed or border, or given a protective covering of peat to minimise the risk of them freezing completely.

In winter, or in spring when late frosts threaten, plants can be protected by carefully wrapping them in a covering of fleece. If there is a heavy snowfall, knock the snow off conifers or other evergreens or their shape could be ruined.

If you live in an area where you can expect harsh winter weather, you could try adding an extra layer of insulation to your pots by lining them with sheets of foam or bubble wrap or with layers of moss before planting. Alternatively, if you use an inner liner pot for planting inside a larger decorative pot, it is an easy job to pack the space between the two pots with insulating material.

PESTS AND DISEASES

Close-packed plantings can succumb to pests and diseases quite rapidly, so it is important that you check your plants regularly.

However, as most container displays are intended to last for only a short period, they may not be around for long enough for any serious problems to build up, and, if they do, the simplest solution is often to throw away the plants and start again. If you decide to re-use the same container, it is essential to clean and disinfect it thoroughly before replanting.

The first essential is to start with healthy plants, and you should avoid introducing problems by checking all the plants that you buy carefully.

Always use fresh compost each time you plant up a container. Throw away old compost rather than re-using it as it may harbour pests and disease.

After this, to keep problems at bay the golden rules are regular care and maintenance, good hygiene and early detection.

Regular feeding and watering will keep your plants healthy and less likely to succumb to pests or diseases. Remove any dying foliage or debris promptly, and keep the area around your pots clean and tidy to limit places for pests to hide.

Check your plants frequently, preferably each time you water them, as problems are more easily dealt with if they are spotted early on. A few greenfly, for example, can easily be removed by hand, without the need to use chemicals, before the pest becomes well established.

If you do find a more serious problem and need to resort to the use of chemical controls, take care to select the most appropriate one, and be sure to follow the manufacturer's instructions carefully. Plant-based extracts are generally the safest substances.

Positioning pots

You will, of course, want to place your containers for the best possible effect. Steps and entrances are more attractive when thriving pot plants are placed beside them. For a classically formal look, position a matched pair of plants in identical pots either side of the front door.

Grouping of potted plants together is often very successful. Groups can be used to create greater impact or to conceal an ugly spot in your garden, and containers of different shapes and sizes can look better when they are grouped together.

For added height, upturn an empty pot and use it as a base for another. Pots with pedestals, or those placed on tall columns, look great when boldly trailing plants such as ivy, ivy geranium or nasturtiums are allowed to cascade from them. One beautiful, well-planted urn on its own can make a stunning focal point in a tiny garden.

Create a pleasant corner by placing attractive containers of colourful flowers around an impromtu stone feature.

Grouping a variety of containers together can be a very successful way to brighten a dull corner.

PROTECTING PLANTS FROM THE WIND

Wind is one of the biggest problems for potted plants. It can dry them out rapidly so that they suffer foliage and root damage. You may need to provide some sort of screening if you want to grow plants in exposed positions: a decorative screen or trellis can cut down the strength of the wind to acceptable levels.

Balconies can be especially windy and pots should be positioned so that they cannot blow over. High stands are particularly unsuitable there.

Hanging plant baskets, wherever they are positioned, should be given protection from drying winds as they are exposed to the drying effect on all sides.

MOVING POTS

An advantage of container gardening is that you can move pots around to create different displays, bringing the best ones forward or moving fading ones out of sight. However, once a large tub has been filled with potting mix, it can be quite difficult to move. Providing the ground has a smooth, even surface, large wooden tubs can be moved more easily when mounted on castors. Alternatively, place a strip of strong carpet under the container and drag it along.

If you have a lot of pots to move and a large area, invest in a two-wheeled trolley. It would also be useful for moving large bags of potting mix, peat moss and fertiliser.

Index

Published by Merehurst Limited, 1999
Ferry House, 51-57 Lacy Road, Putney, London SW15 1PR

Text copyright © Merehurst Limited
Photography copyright © Murdoch Books (except those
listed below)

ISBN S460/1 85391-767-2

Commissioning Editor: Helen Griffin
Series Editor: Graham Strong
Text: Valerie Duncan and Denise Greig
Illustrator: Helen McCosker
Designers: Bill Mason and Lena Lowe
CEO & Publisher: Anne Wilson

Printed in Singapore by Tien Wah Press

PHOTOGRAPHS:

Leigh Clapp: *pp1, 2, 6, 11 bottom, 13 top, 14, 43 bottom centre, 48
bottom, 49, 50, 66, 71*
Densey Clyne: *pp9, 10 bottom, 40 top left and bottom left, 42 top centre
and bottom, 43 top, 45 top left, 46 top left and centre and bottom,
47 top left, 48 top left, 62, 73 top*
Valerie Duncan: *pp86*
Denise Greig: *pp10 top, 11 top, 37 bottom centre, 41 left, centre
and right, 42 top right, 43 bottom right, 45 top right and bottom, 56
top, 57 top centre, 58 top right, 60 bottom, 61 top left
and right, 64 top, 73 bottom, 76 left and right*
Phil Haley: *pp25, 27, 29 top and bottom, 30, 32, 33, 44 bottom left,
55, 58 bottom, 64 bottom*
Stirling Macoboy: *pp56 bottom*
Merehurst: *pp40 bottom right, 57 top right, 60 top right*
Lorna Rose: *pp37 top and bottom left, 38 centre and right, 42 top left, 47
top right and bottom, 48 top right, 58 top left*
Graham Strong: *pp4, 7, 12, 15, 16, 17, 18, 19, 20, 22, 23, 34, 36,
38 top left, 39, 46 top right, 51, 52, 53, 54, 57 top left, 59, 60
top left, 63, 65, 70 top, 74 top left and right, 75, 77, 78, 80,
81, 84, 85, 88, 89, 92, front and back cover*
Gerry Whitmont: *pp37 bottom right, 40 top centre and right, 43 bottom
left, 57 bottom*

Front cover: Early spring container garden with anemones, tulips,
wallflowers and pansies
Title page: Yellow primroses, red tulips and purple pansies